Hail Noble Washington

**Memories of East Chicago (Indiana)
Washington High School**

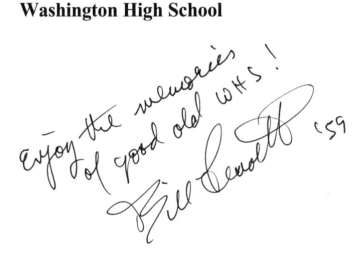

Washington High School Alumni Association

**BookMasters, Inc.
Mansfield, Ohio**

1

ISBN 0-9728853-0-7

Printed in the USA.

BookMasters, Inc.
Mansfield, OH 44905

Book Design by Jeff Hamilton

Table of Contents

Dedication

Frank Hanak   **Archibald McKinlay**

This book is dedicated to Frank Hanak and Archibald McKinlay, whose vision and foresight created the Washington High School Alumni Association. Without their efforts, this book would not have been a reality.

Frank, a Washington graduate of 1938, and Archie, a 1945 grad, gathered a few other Washington alumni shortly after the 60th reunion of the WHS class of 1938 and presented the idea of an alumni association. The timing was right; the enthusiasm of the group was infectious. The first tentative issue of the ANVIL followed shortly thereafter. The successes of the association, its picnics, the homecoming gatherings, the regular monthly issues of the ANVIL, the holiday festivities are a tribute to Frank and Archie.

Frank continues to serve as editor of the ANVIL and chairman of the association.

Preface

This book was published under the auspices of the Washington High School Alumni Association, P.O. Box 505, Griffith, IN 46319. All decisions regarding the content of this book were made by the Core Committee or Book Committee or the WHS Alumni Assn.

Note that most of the content of this book was written by the members of the WHS Alumni Association. We take no responsibility for the accuracy of the information contained, as it is based on the memories of our members. Also, the contents have been edited for consistency of style, to eliminate superfluous information and to fit our space limitations. We apologize to any contributors who think we left out or changed material that was important. We used our best judgment.

The members of the WHS Alumni Assn. Book committee spent countless hours reading through letters and looking at pictures to select the most interesting material to put in this book. Also, members of the committee repeatedly proofread the material, to assure accuracy, readability and consistency of style.

The members of the Book Committee are Bob Krajewski, manager, Bill Leavitt, Ione Williams, Mary Ben, Mary Misirly, Jim Platis and Bette Sedey.

Many members of the WHS Alumni Assn. contributed photos and other memorabilia to this book. For those contributions, we thank them. Also, many others helped immeasurably. Certainly, no one provided more help than Gloria Dosen and the staff in the East Chicago Room at the Indiana Harbor Public Library, or Jeff Hamilton, who typeset and designed this book. We extend our undying gratitude to all those who have helped make this book a success.

-The WHS Alumni Association Book Committee

Introduction—Why This Book?

The Washington High School Alumni Association readily and enthusiastically supported the concept of this book. Most significant for their approval was the notion that we could provide a handy, permanent record of many interesting and entertaining memories and recollections of growing up in the Harbor (Indiana Harbor section of East Chicago, Indiana) and attending Washington High.

We believe the book will help cement stronger bonds between the Association and alums who live outside the region and haven't had the opportunity to attend any of our functions. It's one way of saying thanks for your support.

Some of us have been challenged by friends who can't begin to understand the why and how of our monthly ANVIL, our annual picnic, our homecoming and our holiday party. And now this free book, delivered postage-free to every member!

They ask all kinds of questions: How do you get alums to attend your activities? Why this fundamental attraction to a community that has changed so much? Why don't you grow up and forget your high school days—they're over?

Yes, they are over, but those years were very important years. We grew physically and emotionally; we developed social skills; we participated in all kinds of extra-curricular activities; we began to make career decisions. And the impact of those years is with us still.

Psychologists believe youthful experiences, filtered through one's basic personality structure, make us the persons we are now—with our value systems and our purview of life. Most of us are delighted to have had those experiences in the Harbor and at WHS.

The ANVIL's masthead speaks to keeping our memories alive. Experts in mental health maintain that memories are precious and important. They are bound up with emotions and meanings that help form subsequent attitudes, beliefs and actions. The recall, review and reassessment of happy memories of childhood and adolescence is a meaningful exercise. It leads to self-knowledge, then to the fullness of empathy and then to a greater sense of self-acceptance and self-possession. So, this book is a collection of the happy memories of a great number of WHS alums from many places. We didn't try to replicate the history of East Chicago, and specifically the Harbor; that has been done previously elsewhere. We do offer some vignettes about the Harbor, however. Similarly, our treatment of Washington High's history as relatively cursory— some facts and a lot of memories.

We hope the chapter about WHS principals and teachers leads many to recall at least one or two favorite teachers. Likewise, the sports chapter will remind all of the rich athletic tradition of WHS. Perhaps some readers, in fact, may have attended some of those championship events.

The memories of alums, which are organized by decades beginning with the 1930's, is the heart of the book. These recollections, contributed by our members, it is hoped will amuse you, entertain you and perhaps rekindle some of your own personal, happy memories.

CHAPTER ONE
1
Historical Vignettes of WHS and the Harbor

East Chicago Room

Many an alum has yet to visit the East Chicago Room Museum at the East Chicago Public Library at Alder and Columbus Drive. If you are one of those who has not experienced the pleasure of seeing a vast treasure of our past culture, you're really missing something! There are thousands of photos, documents, books, etc. There are WHS SENIOR ANVILs for every year from 1912 through 1986 as well as several WEEKLY ANVIL's through the years.

Some of the larger collections feature the Indiana Theater, Inland Steel, Boy Scouts, Girl Scouts, City of East Chicago, Katherine House, Col. Riley, Graver Tank, East Chicago Historical Society and St. Catherine's Hospital.

There are oversize photos of athletic teams and hundreds of photos of many buildings, people, churches, etc. There are old telephone directories from 1929 on, and city directories of streets and addresses.

The staff will be glad to assist you in any way. Gloria Dosen is the East Chicago Room Coordinator. Richard Smyers is Senior Reference Librarian, and Michael Piper is the Technical Reference Librarian. Any one of these trained and dedicated persons can help you locate such things as directories of your old neighborhood, information on where you worked, even your old telephone number. There is an extensive census file where you can trace your roots (1840 Census to 1920 Census).

Whether you go to the "Room" to explore or reminisce, you will probably leave with the thought that this might be the place you would donate some of your WHS and/or Harbor memorabilia.

Your treasures will be safe there and will be shared by many for years to come. Give Gloria Dosen a call at 219-397-2453 for any information you may need or any questions you may have about making such donations. A free pick-up service is offered if within a reasonable distance. If you wish to ship your donations directly to the Library, ship to East Chicago History Room, 2401 E. Columbus Dr., East Chicago, IN 46312.

Sharon Bohling, Publicity Coordinator, provided the brochures for inclusion in the ANVIL for alumni. Thank you Sharon. Michael Salvio ('47) of Bridgeport, WV, recently sent eight WEEKLY ANVIL's from the 1937 time period. Some portion of the "1937" column came from him. Thanks Michael.

An early picture of Washington High School

Deodar was a Great Place to Live!

Elsie Moss • Class of 1950 • Highland, IN

The 3700 block of brick-laden Deodar Street: What a great place to live! I know Deodar has been mentioned before, but here are some more names. I lived on the corner of Broadway and Deodar, Third Floor. On this one block alone lived: Rosemarie Garcia, Phillip and Marie Sequeiros, Julie Vargo, the Lucas family, Norma Jean Popoff, Sainato Family, the Bruno family, Hank and Dolores Zawacki, the Nallenweg family and George Hero. Everything was within walking distance. It had to be, no one had a car. Around the corner on Broadway was Boilek's, Arzumanian Market and Dr. Forszt.

Going east toward Main Street was a Chinese Laundry, a fish market, Manta and Hurst (Attny.), The Grill Restaurant; and remember the Taxi Cab office (a tiny, narrow hall-type aisle situated between the Grill and Harbor Pharmacy). Then the 37th block of Main Street—the hub of the Harbor—had everything! The First National Bank, the tallest building, had seven floors loaded with all kinds of doctors, lawyers, etc. Then there was Ellen-A-Dress Shoppe, Father and Son Shoes, Tip Top Shoe Store, Kleinman Drugs on both corners, Newberry and Woolworth Dime Stores (remember the "Evening in Paris" perfume in a blue bottle with a grey tassle?), Harbor Furniture, Goodman Furniture (Twin City), Edward's Store for Men, Buehler Bros. Meat Market, Joe Title & Sons Meat Market, Krogers, Karsch's Bakery, Hot Dog John's (a hole in the wall with the best chili), March Travel Agency, Marcus Jewelers, Simon Miller, and Goulds, the biggest department store.

Hammond had Goldblatts and we had Goulds and Mademoiselle Dress and Bridal Shop with Judy Hanak as the Bridal Consultant. I am enjoying the ANVIL as much as I did in High School. Keep up the great work!

Harold Goodman • Class of 1942 • Los Angeles, CA

The establishment known as Goodman Drug Store, located at Main and Guthrie, was in existence for several years before cousins Bob Goodman ('45) and Martin Goodman ('45) became pharmacists and took over the business. In the mid-fifties the partnership broke up—Martin moved to Los Angeles and Bob took over and ran the store for years later. This business was something of an institution in the area. The clientele was heavily loaded with steel workers and paydays at Inland and Youngstown were the busiest. Paychecks were cashed and payments were made on accounts. The credit records were kept on 5 x 8 cards. Harold Goodman ('42) remembers a group of cards marked Pedro Gomez #1, Pedro Gomez #2, up to Pedro Gomez #6.

Everything from Kessler's whiskey to radio vacuum tubes to "Evening in Paris" toiletry sets was stocked. There was a soda fountain. One banner day was marked by the installation of a two-ton air conditioner; heaven in the hot, humid summers. The true spirit of the store was embodied by George Prieto, a talented and loyal employee who spent his entire adult life with the Goodmans.

Anecdotes: Harold Goodman was allowed to man the cigarette and candy counter at age 13. The premium cigarettes (Lucky Strikes, Camels, Old Golds and Chesterfield) sold two packs for 25 cents. Of course, Wings and Marvels were a cheaper price. On the counter was a wooden box with a glass front. A penny deposited yielded one cigarette. Harold's first customer bought a package of Wrigley's Doublemint gum and gave him a 50-cent piece. He rang up 50 cents instead of a nickel. Cousin Max was unhappy.

Next door was a saloon with Dutch curtains in the front windows. These blocked the view of children on the sidewalk but we knew something evil was going on inside. At Easter time the owner barbequed a whole lamb and opened the door to all the merchants and their kids. Harold remembers platters of fragrant lamb and Greek peppers and has loved lamb ever since.

Across the street on the corner was a "restaurant" that served what we would call chili dogs today. I'm sure they weren't kosher and the sanitation could have been better but we had cast-iron stomachs and Pop would indulge us occasionally. Next door was Frank and George's barber shop. Either one would lift me onto a cushioned board supported by the arms of his barber chair. I liked the smell of Vitalis and talcum powder. They did all my haircuts before I left for college. Farther down Main Street was a shoeshine parlor where Pop's weekly shoeshine was done. I was allowed to sit on his lap to watch the process. They would also block fedoras.

Cement Plant

The old Universal Atlas Cement plant, like so many other things from our past, will soon pass into oblivion.

The 180 acres of lake front property will probably be sold for development into recreational and residential properties surrounding Gary's casino boats.

When Buffington Harbor opened in 1927 with its deepwater harbor, Universal soon became the largest cement manufacturer in the United States.

We don't know how old this is!

The Harbor

Camp Wright is a jungle today. After hearing that the camp was "rotting away," Sylvia and Ed Kuta recently toured the property. Their guide was Ernest Hiatt of Rochester, IN. Ernest, still active in local scouting, was and is a neighbor of the Camp Wright property, having lived on the farm next to the camp since he was a child in the 1930s. He is probably the foremost authority on the camp today. If anyone has any questions or wants any information, contact Ernest at 3404 West 450 North, Rochester, IN 46975 (Phone 219-223-3232).

On this tour, which seemed like it lasted most of the day, the Kutas walked through dense growth that looked like the Tarzan jungle scenes we used to see at the Indiana Theatre. Brush was everywhere, trees grown up to the sky, fallen dead branches, everything except the swinging vines. Remember how Johnny Weissmuller always found the next vine "right there" when he was finished with the last one? But, that's another story. There were no animals we could see lurking in this jungle with the exception of one deer dashing some 30 feet in front of us and startling us a little.

Ernest pointed out where the boys' huts stood. Only one pile of rotted lumber from one hut is visible today. The ball field, the parking lot, the trails, the river bank, everything is covered by overgrown vegetation. Only part of a bridge is intact and that's because it was made from Indiana Harbor steel.

One urinal stands in the growth—a reminder of what was in its time the state-of-art sanitary facilities. The ice house and the leaders' huts have only the block foundations showing with a few rotting planks around.

The only building still standing is the Dining Hall and Kitchen. This, too, was built of Harbor steel. Parts of the hall have rusted away. However, the wire over the river is still in place.

Harold "Flash" Taylor ('47) has movie films of Camp Wright taken by Carl Johnson in 1938, 1939 and 1940. If any one is interested in these films, contact Flash at 219-996-6571 or 799 West 750 South, Hebron, IN 46341.

Photographs of the present day campsite are available for viewing at the East Chicago Room Museum along with programs, directories, etc. [Note: In the 1950s, the Rochester Camp Wright was replaced by another Camp Wright (called William Wright Scout Reservation) in Westville, Indiana. This camp Wright was in use through the 1950s.]

Hoosier Boy Scouts

Harold Goodman • Class of 1942 • Los Angeles, CA

I have a few fairly clear memories of boy scout camp. It was outside Rochester, Indiana, next to a cornfield. The Tippecanoe River ran nearby.

I'd never been that far from home before. We were transported on the back of an open truck. What a thrill! I remember weeping willows overhanging the river bank and hearing stories of General Tyler. I didn't actually fall out of a canoe so that was a benign fib.

Meals were in a big mess hall and one morning at breakfast we were told that Wylie Post and Will Rogers had died in a plane crash. We all knew about the famous pilot who wore an eye patch and the beloved comedian. That saddened us.

The camp counselors told ghost stories around a night campfire and we played a game of some sort creeping in the dark through rows of corn. I guess the farmer liked kids.

Our troop met in the basement of a church on Guthrie. I made second class scout but could get no higher. This was the middle of the 1930s. We were not too concerned about the Great Depression.

One of my favorite authors is Mark Twain. Having read his novels, speeches and articles, I come down on "Life on the Mississippi" as the most enjoyable, and intend to reread it. Fibber McGee had it down perfectly. Mark Twain's favorite target was politicians. Mine too!

Another Landmark Is Toppled

East Chicago's first skyscraper, our landmark Union National Bank Building, located at Main and Broadway, has had its top half "sliced off" in 1999. The building is being downsized to a three- story structure. It will still house a bank. Sure it will be nice, but not as beautiful as the original bank building was when it opened in 1929.

Do you remember the massive main floor with its imported Italian marble walls, floors of terrazzo with brass strips, the massive bronze chandeliers? The huge safe deposit vault? The high-speed Otis elevator?

Many of us, as youngsters, had passbook savings accounts at that bank. If you were one of those depositors then, do you remember receiving a small oval shaped chrome bank with a handle in which to save your coins? After this child's bank was full you took it to one of the cashiers (safely tucked inside her cage). She counted your coins and entered the amount in your passbook, and sometimes she entered your earnings interest. Didn't you feel proud of yourself?

Remember riding up in that elevator (a pleasure) to Dr. Jarabak's office to have your cavities drilled (definitely not a pleasure), and then riding down again? What a pleasure to make it out of "that" chair!

Space in this column restricts mentioning all the law offices, doctors' offices and insurance and real estate offices that occupied the top five floors.

Col. Riley must be rolling over several times in his grave during this remodeling!

Driving down Columbus Drive in mid-June I saw the building that housed "our" bowling alley being bulldozed. But, that's another story.

The Founding of St. Catherine's Hospital

Frank Hanak • Class of 1938 • Griffith, IN

In a recent conversation with an ANVIL reporter, Lawrence Mervis, class of 1942, Mervis said that his father was the driving force in getting the hospital built. His father, Dr. Frank H. Mervis, was a jovial, normal-sized man, who loved people and the Harbor. He arrived in the Harbor in 1914. He had a great practice. There was only one problem, there was no hospital in the Harbor. The only local hospitals were St. Margaret's in Hammond and Mercy Hospital in Gary.

In 1924, he went to the Archbishop in Fort Wayne to see about building a hospital in the Harbor. The good Archbishop was in favor but told Dr. Mervis if he could come up with $750,000, the Catholic Church would consider the hospital being built. (Note: $750,000 in 1924 is equivalent to approximately $5,000,000 today!) After much thinking and asking, Dr. Mervis approached Inland Steel Company brothers P. D. & E. J. Block for a contribution. They agreed to donate the money and the land with the stipulation that it be kept a secret. The rest is history. The Archbishop assigned the German order of nuns, The Poor Handmaidens of Jesus Christ as the administrators. They still administer to this excellent hospital.

The St. Catherine's Hospital was dedicated in April of 1927 to the glory of God and our friend Dr. Frank H. Mervis. If you wish to contact Lawrence Mervis, call 1-800-393-8444. He welcomes calls from the Region Alumni.

Sounds of Indiana Harbor

Bill Leavitt • Class of 1959 • Merrillville, IN

Sometimes, during a quiet night in my suburban home, I imagine a fog horn or the powerful "booms" of the hammers at Standard Forging or Indiana Forge in the Indiana Harbor of my youth. Those of us who grew up in Indiana Harbor, especially those who lived north of Columbus Drive became familiar with the sounds that were unique to the "Harbor." The foghorn and the hammers are the first things I think of when I think back to the sounds at night. But also there were the bells at St. Francis Catholic Church, a half-block from my Fir Street home, and the train whistles and the rumble of trains that you could feel and hear. I also remember the bell of the knife sharpener and the whistles from the mills.

I discussed these sounds with fellow WHS alumni at the recent WHS Alumni Assn. Holiday Festival. My tablemates added some other unique sounds that may be familiar to various alumni, depending on your age group: The wind whistle to signal high winds at the mills; the shouts of the "Rags and Iron" man, the fruit man, the junk man, the ice man and the tamale man; the call of the "bedbug" man; an finally the bells at WHS warning that school would soon start.

I'm sure each of us remembers a different combination of sounds, but I bet you haven't found any other place that produces the same sounds. Next time you are in a quiet place, think back to your childhood and concentrate—you just might hear some of those sounds again.

Anna (Torres) Vasquez, left, Stella (Torres) Garber and Robert Botello are all members of a Mexican-American family which attended WHS and served honorably in the Air Force.

Indiana Harbor Families

Bill Leavitt • Class of 1959 • Merrillville, IN

Many Indiana Harbor families had multiple generations attend WHS. An interesting example of that is Anna (Torres) Vasquez, who attended WHS until she was married in 1937. She was the first of three Mexican-American family members to serve in the Air Force.

Anna entered the Air Force during World War II, in 1942. She left two children at home and joined the WACs

(Women's Air Corps), serving in Orlando, Florida, training Allied squadrons from Great Britain, Russia, Scotland, Mexico and the U.S. Anna's sister, Stella (Torres) Garber, who also attended WHS, was in the Air Force during the Korean War. Anna's son, Robert Botello, was in the WHS class of 1960. He also entered the Air Force, serving during the time of the Cuban Missile Crisis.

Walking In the Harbor

Bob Krajewski • Class of 1946 • Munster, IN

While browsing through some bed-time reading material, I came across two related bits of information that led me to reflect on an aspect of my Riley School and WHS days and the incredible societal changes we've seen since then.

Those two items treated the number of automobiles in the U.S. and the amount of walking done by the average American. The first item reported that over 19 million new cars were sold in the U.S. and there are now well over 200 million on our roads. The second item commented on our walking habits and revealed the average American walks less than 75 miles a year. Initially, that seems like a lot; however, when it's broken down, that's about 1.4 miles a week, or barely 350 yards a day.

I reflected on how many miles I must have walked as an elementary and high school pupil.

Occasionally, when I now drive past a school at dismissal time, I am stunned at the number of cars—parents picking up their children—and in the case of high schools, the area devoted to student parking. In my entire E.C. Schools career, I was never driven to regular school classes. To be fair, most of that time my folks didn't have a car. Even when they did, however, a ride to school was not to be expected. I lived about six blocks from WHS and in four years, I walked home for lunch every day, as almost all of us did in the 1942-1946 era. If there was something such as a school cafeteria, I was totally unaware of it.

My walk home was a brisk ten minutes or so, a snap; some of my classmates who lived at the extremes of the Harbor and Calumet sections also made that lunch walk daily. Surely they had but time for a quick sandwich or a bowl of soup and a glass of milk. Again, that's what many of us had.

It seems almost everyone I knew walked everywhere—family visits, recreational sites, shopping and just walking for the simple pleasure of it. WWII was part of it, of course. The three gallons a week from an "A" stamp wasn't very much; those precious stamps had to be saved for special occasions.

In retrospect, I am always amazed that the Harbor was seen by all as so safe for walking. Even young girls and women of all ages had no fear of walking absolutely everywhere at any time. For example, for many of us a walk to Larry's at the corner of Michigan and Guthrie to check out the scene was almost a nightly assignment. And the girls showed up in two's and three's, from all over town. Remember how crowded Larry's and the Spot were after football and basketball games?

For many of today's teenagers, hangouts are their area's shopping mall, but they have to drive to get there.

Much of the decline in walking in all urban areas is due to the increase in street crime. That's a situational issue; where you live is a factor. Times change.

America's love affair with the automobile can be demonstrated by the decline of Main Street as a shopping center. In the 1930s and 1940s, it was thronged with shoppers. As more were able to buy cars, they shopped elsewhere.

An attempt to resurrect it as a pedestrian-only-mall was a failed experiment. That failure too has been replicated across

America.

Currently, I still walk the golf course and hike to the library whenever my arthritis is under control. But, I must quit now; I have to jump in the car to pick up a couple of things at the grocery.

East Chicago High School Building, Magoun Avenue and 144th Street, as it appeared in 1900. The building later became Harrison School.

Washington High School History
1948 Senior Anvil*

The second class ever to leave the East Chicago High School was graduating that Thursday evening, June 1899. There were three graduates, one less than the preceding year. Those graduates had attended a school very different from any that exist today. More than likely, they had begun their studies in the two-room Township High School that stood at 145th and Northcote.

Then, in 1898, the scholars had moved to the Tod Opera House as the city took over the high school. They studied on the third floor of the building every day from 8:00 am until 3:00 pm. The staff—Miss Bronson, teacher of history and Latin; Miss Lyons, teacher of English; and Mr. Slocomb, principal and teacher of mathematics and science—taught in three rooms. One of these rooms seated all the pupils, so it was used for a study hall. The other two rooms were used alternately by the three teachers.

A definite amount of work was required, although there was no credit system. The graduates received grades given on the percentage basis and were given little encouragement in the form of scholarships; however, when a student seemed to have the initiative and intelligence to continue his or her education, the teachers urged the parents to send him or her on.

These were the conditions under which students received their education while the East Chicago High School was in the making.

The town grew, and when a town grows, the high school must also grow. The small space in the Opera House because unbearably overcrowded. Plans were made. A new high school for East Chicago was to be built! East Chicago residents were very enthusiastic as they attended the dedicatory exercises that evening of 1900.

The building still stands [as of 1948]; although it is now called the Harrison Building.

This was not the place to stop, though, for now the other side of town was growing. The authorities decided that another school should be built. In 1903, the building, which eventually became the Washington Elementary School, was started. The year 1908 found this building, at the corner of Columbus Drive and Parrish Avenue, complete and ready for use. It was used as a grade school until 1912. Then the East Chicago High School moved in, and along with the Harrison Building it was used to educate high school students.

The first class was graduated from the East Chicago High School building at Columbus Drive and Parrish Avenue in 1914. The buildings to the north of it between Hemlock Street and Parrish Avenue were started in 1918 and completed in 1921. The year 1925 found the city needing another high school. This new high school would become Roosevelt High School.

Since there were to be two high schools, there could no longer simply be an East Chicago High School. The new school on the west side of town was named Roosevelt and the old one on the east side, Washington. The modern building on Parrish Avenue was added in 1939 to complete the high school block. As if to prove its need of this building, the school reached the highest number of graduates in June of 1941 with 432 graduating.

Washington is still growing; perhaps not in number of pupils, but in conveniences and modern methods of teaching. We are proud of 50 years of the best in high schools— Washington of East Chicago!

*This is a school history that was written and printed in the 1948 SENIOR ANVIL. We thought you would enjoy it. Slight editing changes were made to the original text to eliminate confusion with dates and make it more understandable.

CHAPTER TWO
2
The Alumni Association

The Beginnings of the WHS Alumni Association

Many WHS alums wonder how the WHS Alumni Association got its start. In August, 1998, the class of 1938 was having its 60th Reunion. Joe Siminski, committee president, asked Frank Hanak to be the speaker. Frank declined because the six previous reunion speakers passed away (an omen?). Joe insisted Frank get a replacement speaker. Frank contacted Archibald McKinlay ('45) and Archie consented to serve as guest speaker. He presented the class members with a complimentary copy of his book "Reejin Archetypes."

A few days later Archie called Frank with an idea. He said he had seen so much good will, friendly spirit, love and compassion at the Class of 1938 reunion that he felt perhaps many, if not all, former classmates would feel the same.

It was decided that Frank would organize an alumni committee and Archie would write a monthly replica of the weekly ANVIL. Archie was in the process of writing three books and daily articles for "The Times' Millennium Series." For assistance, he called upon his wife, Pat, to typeset ANVIL copy; upon Ed Kuta ('45) to handle the printing; then upon Sylvia (Kuzman '46) Kuta to distribute the copies.

After five issues of the new ANVIL, Archie resigned as acting editor. Sylvia was coaxed into becoming the new editor. In organizing the membership list, Sylvia, with some help from committee members, has mailed approximately 10,500 ANVILs to date.

In its first year, The WHS Alumni Association sponsored three well-attended events: The 1998 Holiday Buffet, the

First Annual Homecoming and the party-within-a-party with the E.C. Hall of Fame Dinner. Currently, the WHS Alumni Association sponsors two dinners and a picnic each year.

The purpose of the WHS Alumni Association is to keep the Washington High School name alive, provide members with news and entertainment, and create a sense of community for all participants. The high school was torn down in 1986.

The Alumni Association publishes a newsletter, The ANVIL, which readers may notice resembles the product that once rolled out of Mr. Altenderfer's print shop every week. The alumni ANVIL comes out monthly.

The original managing core group has been headed by Frank Hanak ('38), and includes Ed Kuta ('45), Sylvia Kuzman (Kuta) ('46), Dick Rudzinski, ('44), Gwen Sargent ('38), Irma Jean Romer (Rader) ('41), Alex Soverly ('38), Mary Benn ('36), Helen Lucas ('38), Leo Miller ('34), Joseph Siminski ('38), Ione Williams ('38), Lillian Fry ('38), Walter Kempera ('38) and Archibald McKinlay ('45). Since its beginning other members have joined this core group.

The Alumni ANVIL

The monthly ANVIL is a vehicle intended to keep members abreast of other WHS Alumni while preserving the WHS name and notifying members of alumni events. The ANVIL is supported by donations.

But what of The ANVIL itself ? While East Chicago High School was still in the Harrison building (1900-14), The LOTUS came into existence as the school's yearbook, and, in 1917, two years after the high school moved to Indiana Harbor, a single sheet, called The ANVIL, replaced it as a monthly magazine. By the fattened final edition of The ANVIL in 1920, the so-called magazine looked suspiciously like a yearbook.

So, in 1921, following the high school's moving from

what became the Washington Elementary and Junior High building into the first of the new Washington High School buildings, the monthly ANVIL was split into two publications having the same name. The enlarged annual version became the SENIOR ANVIL, the school's yearbook, while the periodical became The ANVIL, a weekly news publication.

Prior to 1930, The ANVIL was written by the journalism class, the members of the ANVIL staff being chosen at the end of each semester by the instructor, Viola Hoffman. The little newspaper was typeset and run off by the printing classes, presided over by T.V. Altenderfer. With The Great Depression at hand in 1930, however, The ANVIL temporarily was printed in the Tuesday edition of the "Calumet News." It soon returned to the school print shop.

In 1939, a shock tremor rolled through WHS when it was announced that Grace Papp would be editor-in-chief of the paper. Reaction was swift. Indignant boys demanded to know, "What does a girl know about running a paper?" "It can't possibly be done." Would-be WHS career girls shot back, "A girl to manage things around here is just what we need. It can be done, and Grace will prove it." As usual, the girls were right.

Week after week The ANVIL appeared edited with a fine precision, as Grace's finesse with a blue pencil set a new standard of achievement. Five years later, that standard was raised by another female editor. Margaret Horn would hold down the position of editor-in-chief for most of two consecutive years (1944-45 and 1945-46), and would consolidate all the progress that had been made during the previous almost three decades.

[Note: Sometime in the 1950s, the weekly newsletter's name was changed to the SENATORIAL.]

Miss Washington

Six Miss East Chicago Washingtons by decades were selected at the WHS Alumni Association third Annual Homecoming at Villa Cesare in Schererville on February 18, 2001. Left to right: 1920s—Jean Templeton ('26); 1930s—Mary Ben ('36); 1940s—Sophie Medrea Marravilla ('40); 1950s—Bette Sedey ('50); 1960s—Lynn Garaffa (Bloom) ('61); 1970s—Christine Russell ('74). Archibald McKinlay ('45) presented the flowers to each Miss Washington, and his wife, Pat, assisted by pinning the Miss Washington banners. Frank Hanak and Mario Martini were project managers.

WHS Alumni Assn. Core Committee

A group picture of the current core committee of your Alumni Association was taken in September, 2002. Members are, seated left to right: Erma Jean (Romer) Rader ('41), Mary Ben ('36), Jo (Gustaitis) Booth ('34), Ione Williams ('38), Vera (Markovich) Heralovich ('38), Jean Templeton ('26), Narcissa (Perez) Castillo ('47) and Gloria (Guerro) Fraire ('42). Standing: Jean (McClure) Williams ('44), Joan (Morris) Williams ('50), Bill Leavitt ('59), Walter (Dudzinski) Dee ('40), Bob Krajewski ('46), Bette (Ferencz) Sedey ('50), Christine Russell ('74) and James Platis ('45). Frank Hanak, Ricky Gonzales and Ed Prusiecki were unable to attend the photo shoot.

WHS Alumni Association Takes Off With a Bang

Archibald McKinlay • Class of 1945 • Chicago, IL

A little over four years ago, just before the holiday season (Oct. 18, 1998), I announced in this column that I was spearheading a movement to create an East Chicago Washington Alumni Association. Since four years is a normal academic cycle, I think I now owe it to you to report on how the venture fared. To use, or misuse, a show biz term, it's been buffo!

Everything about the association has been successful, and it has added to the happiness of many people throughout the Calumet Region, and beyond. Indeed, people who went to other Calumet Region high schools have inquired about how to start an association, and the East Chicago Washington group has freely shared information. Some East Chicago Roosevelt Alums even have suggested that they be allowed to be members, but, of course, that is out of the question.. Allowing an RHS (Remedial High School) alum into a WHS meeting would be like filling up the gas tank while smoking a fire cracker.

But I can share lessons learned. The first is that luck plays an important part in the formation of an alumni association. In our case, luck is spelled H-a-n-a-k. I had spoken to a reunion of the class of 1938 and afterward said to Frank Hanak, the person who invited me to speak, that it was a shame the evening's warm, fuzzy feeling could not be replicated. Later, I thought to myself "Why not?" So I went back to Frank, and things began to happen. Frank was a whirling dervish. He organized the core group and ever since has been its driving force, until he recently took a deserved break. For the past four years, Frank's living room in Griffith has resembled a paper recycling plant without the recycler.

One of the really intelligent things we did was to revive our school newspaper, the ANVIL. To get it started, I wrote the prototype and first five editions, while Ed Kuta ('45) of Bourbonnais had it printed and his wife, the former Sylvia Kuzman ('46), handled distribution and correspondence. Jim Platis ('45) wrote the sports page and still does. Eventually, Ed and Sylvia took over the editorial function, too, before turning it over to Mario Martino ('59) of Munster. When Mario's business prevented him from continuing, Frank Hanak backstopped him, and presently, Bob Krajewski, long-time superintendent of East Chicago schools has tackled the assignment.

In the ANVIL, news relating to association activities appears alongside information that recalls for readers activities of the late school. And there's plenty of the later. What helps make that relatively easy is the fact that, according to an informed alum with a long memory, East Chicago Washington was once (about 1937) considered to be the best high school in the United States. It was way ahead of the pack on such activities as: a junior college (first one in the state); Paul Robeson Glee Club (African-American singing group); student advisers (Washington Brothers and Girl's Counselors); weight-lifting team (only one in the state); and Girl's Band (only one in the state and one of only two in the Midwest).

We also decided to have events throughout the year. The Holiday Festival from 1 to 5 p.m. December 30, 2002 at Wicker Park social Center was the fifth edition. The first one took place at beautiful Woodmar Country Club and was managed by Gwen Sargent ('38), Richard Seto ('53), Ione Williams ('38) and me, buttressed by Irma Jean Romer (Rader) and Mary Ben (Young) ('36). It was a smash hit, as was the next one, but as more and more alumni participated, Woodmar quickly became too small. Also, alumni began to come in from all over the country—from Florida to California, Montana to Arizona.

Other events have included: Homecoming (on Washington's birthday—get it?), the East Chicago Hall of Fame banquet, a summer picnic and directory. Future events may include a film festival featuring movie stars who attended Washington High School, and a book on WHS that will go to all members.

From the Indiana State University Alumni Association, Terre Haute, IN

Frank, Thank you for sharing the news clippings and the copy of the ANVIL. Congratulations on the success of the E.C. Washington Alumni Association!

You, Mary Sufana, Frank Kollintzas, Jake Arzumanian, Bob Krajewski, Coach Baratto, and hundreds of other E. C. Washington alumni and teachers graduated from Indiana State. We're proud of all of you, and appreciate your continuing interest and friendship.

Please accept the enclosed check as a token of the high regard we have for the contributions to society made by the alumni and teachers of East Chicago Washington High School. Best wishes from Indiana State University, John P. Newton, Executive Director Alumni Affairs.

Captain Underpants: Tips on How to Write for the ANVIL

Bob Krajewski • Class of 1946 • Munster, IN

Some of our readers keep telling us that they can't easily handle the rush of memories they have about the Harbor and WHS when they try to write something for the ANVIL. There are so many memories and recollections that come to mind that they feel swamped and can't put anything together. That mindset is understandable, but there is a way to work through that problem. The story is in the details!

Yes, a good anecdote about WHS or the Harbor is in the details and how you respond to them. Allow me to illustrate.

Every week I scan the fiction bestseller lists to make certain I've not missed the latest whodunit or suspense thriller. There are no little ones around so I usually don't bother with the children's list. However, I recently noticed a blurb touting the author who created "Captain Underpants." A book on the children's list was titled "Captain Underpants and the Wrath of the Wicked Wedgie Woman." The Wicked Wedgie Woman? Captain Underpants?

I should read that book to discover, for me, the new Captain Underpants, but that would perhaps erase my illusions, my memories, my recollections of

ground chants by jump roping girls on the playgrounds at Riley School at recess and before and after school. The blacktop and sidewalks at Riley seemed to be full of jumping, twisting, gyrating girls rhythmically chanting in sync with the slap-slap-slap of the rope. In the early evening, in decent weather, one would see groups rope jumping whenever at least three girls met seemingly anywhere in the Harbor. For a decade I was an itinerant speech pathologist in and out of elementary schools, so I was aware of kid's activities. But that was a long time ago. Do they still jump rope as they used to? Are there any new rhymes to go with a jumping cadence?

And, in this day and age, I am not about to hang around an elementary school to conduct that kind of research!

Or is that activity gone with the loss of neighborhood camaraderie and sitting on the front porch or the apartment's front stoop chatting with all who strolled by? I'm afraid so.

But the point of the exercise is to illustrate how you can take just one small detail of your current lifestyle, relate it to what you recall about the Harbor or WHS, add your personal reactions about what you felt, thought or did, and you have a great anecdote for the ANVIL. And so, I give a hand salute to Captain Underpants!

Where Are They Now

Slightly more than 65% of the members of the WHS Alumni Association live in the Calumet Region or nearby. The remainder are scattered across the USA. Here is a breakdown of where the membership alums reside as of 2001.

Alabama - 3	Mississippi - 2
Arizona - 25	Montana - 3
Arkansas - 3	North Carolina - 2
California - 55	North Dakota - 1
Colorado - 12	Nebraska - 2
Connecticut - 3	New Jersey - 2
Florida - 51	New Mexico - 3
Georgia - 4	Nevada - 7
Hawaii - 2	New York - 2
Idaho - 2	Ohio - 12
Illinois - 75	Oregon - 3
Indiana - 703	Pennsylvania - 4
Kentucky - 1	South Carolina - 2
Louisiana - 1	Tennessee - 3
Massachusetts - 1	Texas - 16
Maryland - 5	Virginia - 3
Michigan - 17	Washington - 4
Minnesota - 3	Wisconsin - 9
Missouri - 3	

CHAPTER THREE

3
What Was Special About the Harbor and WHS?

Bill Leavitt • Class of 1959 • Merrillville, IN

The experience of forty years since graduating from East Chicago Washington High School has given me a certain amount of wisdom. All my life I suspected that growing up and going to school in Indiana Harbor was a unique experience. However, everyone else I knew from other towns said their experience was novel too.

However, now I know I was right. The difference between Indiana Harbor (and Washington High School) and every other town or city and school was that Indiana Harbor was a blue-collar town filled with every race, nationality and religion there is. But what does that mean to kids who grew up there?

Well, first we all knew it meant that most people worked hard for a living. They worked hard and they got dirty. They were tired. And they didn't get much more money than they needed to get by. But they were proud, proud that they made products that were basic to America. The other thing that kids learned was that society was made up of a lot of different kinds of people. And there wasn't much difference between them.

I went to school with people of something like 50 different nationalities, religions and races. There was no majority in our school—only a lot of minorities. My closest friends were black, white and Hispanic (Mexican); they were Catholic, Protestant, Orthodox and Jewish; they were Serbian, Polish, Croatian and Chinese. Some of them were other religions and nationalities I didn't know about at that time. Most of them are still my friends today. One thing I didn't learn about was prejudice. I was taught that later, but it didn't take.

What I did learn was how to get along with a lot of different kinds of people. I learned that most people (of all kinds) are honorable, kind and caring. If you start out treating people the way you want to be treated, you'll get along just fine nearly all the time.

The ability to get along with people has served me well in my life. It was a long time before I realized how important a lesson it was. Many others from the Harbor and WHS have expressed the same appreciation.

For many of us, that is the best memory from childhood—that it was so easy to get along with lots of different kinds of people in our hometown in those days. Everyone seemed to WANT TO GET ALONG. It's not so easy in today's complicated society, but my WHS lessons have helped me to get along better than most people.

Harborite by Osmosis

Samuel Weinstein, Science Supervisor, E. C. Washington Highland, IN

Enclosed is another contribution to help keep going in those great efforts that keep us all focused on those great years at WHS. They were "vintage" years, yours and mine. You know, contrary to what you may think, one does not have to have been born and/or reared in the Harbor (that wonderful spot) to be a Harborite. One can achieve it by hard work or even by a kind of osmosis.

I was born and reared in New Haven, Connecticut, and got to this "golden land" via WWII, the G.I. Bill and Purdue, West Lafayette. When I compared growing up notes with my colleagues (born and bred Harborites) I found that my growing-up-years were a lot like theirs (a golden age).

This even went as far as using the same techniques for sneaking into the many movie palaces that dotted the place. Years later, in a group of colleagues when one said to me, "Well, you know, you grew up in the Harbor too," I knew I had "arrived."

My wife Eva (who also was born and reared in New Haven, CT) and I appreciate your efforts to keep those WHS memories alive. They were truly "vintage" years. So it's a sincere "well done" and "keep on trucking!"

Myrna Lewis (Goldsmith) • Class of 1959 • Hoffman Estates, IL

Art and I thoroughly enjoy the ANVIL. What a wonderful job the staff does.

My life has been as exciting as anyone could experience. The greatest stories I share are those of the Harbor. My background was developed then, and the unique qualities acquired seemed to create a career for me with juvenile offenders and gangs. You see, we all learned through our "roots" in the Harbor, nothing should be disposable. Apply that philosophy to youth in crisis and we will bring the children back.

To all of our WHS "family:" Health and Happiness in the next year and in those to follow.

Harold Goodman • Class of 1942 • Los Angeles, CA

Some are calling ours "The Greatest Generation." Perhaps so. The young people who attended Washington High School during the middle third of the last century were blessed in my view, with helping it become so.

That takes nothing away from Roosevelt or Hammond High, I reluctantly admit. There was something unique about Indiana Harbor and the surrounding communities.

A thousand stories can be told about the history of

families that came to the Harbor in the earlier years to escape poverty or oppression. Many brought special skills. Almost all brought religions, attitudes and traditions very different than each other. Something, in each case, made them move in and adapt. The result was that their children, we, became members of the great generation.

The Harbor became a small and early sample of the melting pot that is still evolving in this country. How do you explain the fondness we feel for the high school? Well, our parents, the taxpayers, local industries and politicians saw to it that the very best educational opportunities were provided. The curriculum was rich; extracurricular activities abounded. Sports were encouraged. They even let girls play field hockey in green bloomers. We had ice skating, a swimming pool, glee clubs, orchestra, bands, debate teams, plays, student government, The ANVIL, print shop, wood shop, auto shop. Home economics? Sure. Creative writing? Sure.

"Hail Noble Washington" was second only to the "Star Spangled Banner" and we meant it. We were way ahead of most of the country. An African-American girl was the valedictorian of the class of 1942.

Am I painting too rosy a picture? I don't think so. Frank Hanak and the ANVIL staff are giving generations of graduates the opportunity to keep those days alive. As for the town, it had its rough edges. Al Capone found shelter in the Harbor when things got too hot for his organization in Chicago. For a while we took John Dillinger unto our bosoms. You wanted to flirt with Lady Luck? Try the back room of any cigar store. Cal City was a short bus ride away. Two packs of Lucky Strikes cost 25¢ and the truant officer passed the B.A.B. on his regular rounds. The taverns had Dutch curtains covering the lower half of the windows to keep children from peeking in.

There was an aged lion in the Washington Park Zoo. If

you got too close he had a nasty habit of turning his back and spraying the unsuspecting. Slides and swings in the playground. There was a softball diamond. Polywogs and sunfish and cattails were available in the prairie next to St. Catherine's Hospital. The library had a large children's section in the basement.

The circus came to town once a year and the carnival featured hootchy-cootchy dancers. No kids allowed. Cotton candy. A Gypsy woman would tell your fortune if you had a nickel. The old shell game provided a lesson that the school wouldn't teach.

We had everything including smoke from the mills and Harbor beach next to Inland. All in all, it was pretty OK. And yet Indiana Harbor was much like the rest of the country. We all believed in Santa Claus and The Tooth Fairy until the rude awakening.

Free dishes were given away at the Indiana Theater on special nights; much as was done at movie houses everywhere. We used the common currency which was acceptable in Chicago across the line. Our steel was used in Detroit, far away, without having to pay import duties. We grew athletes and war heroes who were celebrated nationwide.

The Comer Wave
(Kudos to the Washington Faculties)

Norm Comer • Class of 1954 • East Chicago, IN

Seldom has the arrival of one family into a school setting where they all attended the same school, Washington Elementary and Washington High School, and where they all basically had the same teachers throughout, been so fruitful in its results.

James, Norman, Charles and Thelma after attending East Chicago schools thirteen years graduated in 1952, 1954, 1955 and 1956.

Their approach to schooling was like a relentless wave descending on an institution of learning. The very strong and positive motivation came from a woman who lacked any formal education, but having had all her children after reaching the age of thirty, was well schooled in the proper raising of children.

Her outlook for the raising of her children was manifested in years as a domestic worker who not only did credible work for others but learned on the job by observing people around her focusing especially on the raising of the their children and positive outlook on life that so many back in her neighborhood lacked. All of this chronicled in a book by Dr. James Comer entitled "Maggie's American Dream."

Also, my father, Hugh Comer, lent a strong and helping hand in the rearing of the children. He was the strong, silent type who worked as a laborer all his life, but encouraged his children to go beyond what they saw around them. He had great faith in his religion, and in spite of certain vestiges of segregation, he always assured us that the man's day was coming when he could be viewed as any other striving American citizen.

By way of what began with those fine teachers the Comer children now hold thirteen college degrees from colleges whose names my mother could neither read nor spell. By way of summary James has degrees from Indiana University, Howard University, University of Michigan and Yale University where he now serves as the Associate Dean of the Yale Medical College.

Norman has degrees from Northwestern University, Indiana University and Loyola University where he earned his Doctorate and later became Superintendent of the East Chicago Schools.

Charles has two degrees from Indiana University with a second being a degree in Optometry in a profession in which he served as past president of the National Optometrist Association.

Thelma has two degrees from Indiana University and is currently serving as principal at Field Elementary School.

Louise, an older stepsister, retired from the East Chicago schools having taught Elementary Education and French for more than forty years. She also attended WHS many years earlier and was an honor student.

The wave that hit Washington High School was one that is hard to describe other than that somewhere my mother spent numerous hours praying for the strength from above after my father passed away when the eldest of the four had yet to turn twenty years old.

Yes, certainly her prayers were answered.

Remember*

When the worst thing you could do at school was smoke in the bathrooms, flunk a test or chew gum? And the banquets were in the cafeteria and we danced to a juke box later, and all the girls wore fluffy pastel gowns and the boys wore suits for the first time and we were allowed to stay out till 12 pm?

When a '57 Chevy was everyone's dream car . . . to cruise, peel out, lay rubber and watch drag races, and people went steady and girls wore a class ring with an inch of wrapped dental floss or yarn coated with pastel frost nail polish so it would fit her finger?

And no one ever asked where the car keys were 'cause they were always in the car, in the ignition, and the doors were never locked. And you got in big trouble if you accidentally locked the doors at home, since no one ever had a key.

Lying on your back on the grass with your friends and saying things like "That cloud looks like a . . . "? And playing baseball with no adults to help kids with the rules of the game. Back then, baseball was not a psychological group learning experience—it was a game?

Remember when stuff from the store came without safety caps and hermetic seals 'cause no one had yet tried to poison a perfect stranger?

And . . . with all our progress . . . don't you just wish . . . just once . . . you could slip back in time and savor the slower pace . . . and share it with the children of the 1980s and 1990s?

Can you still remember Nancy Drew, The Hardy Boys, Laurel & Hardy, Howdy Doody and The Peanut Gallery, The Lone Ranger, The Shadow Knows, Nellie Belle, Roy and Dale, Trigger and Buttermilk, as well as the sound of a real mower on Saturday morning, and summers filled with bike rides, playing in cowboy land, baseball games, bowling and visits to the pool . . . and eating Kool-Aid powder with sugar?

When being sent to the principal's office was nothing compared to the fate that awaited a misbehaving student at home? Basically, we were in fear for our lives, but it wasn't because of drive by shootings, drugs, gangs, etc. Our parents and grandparents were a much bigger threat! But we all survived because their love was greater than the threat.

Didn't that feel good, just to go back and say, "Yeah, I remember that And was it really that long ago?

Man, I Am Old! How Many Do You Remember??*

Head lights dimmer switches on the floor.
Ignition switches on the dashboard.
Engine starters on the floor.
Heaters mounted on the inside of the fire wall.
Real ice boxes [ask your Mom about that].
Pant leg clips for bicycles without chain guards.
Soldering irons you heat on a gas burner.
Using hand signals for cars without turn signals.

Older Than Dirt Quiz*

Count all the ones that you remember—not the ones you were told about! Ratings at the bottom.

1. Blackjack chewing gum
2. Wax Coke-shaped bottles with colored sugar water
3. Candy cigarettes
4. Soda pop machines that dispensed bottles
5. Coffee shops with tableside jukeboxes
6. Home milk delivery in glass bottles with cardboard stoppers
7. Party lines
8. Newsreels before the movie
9. P. F. Flyers
10. Butch wax
11. Telephone numbers with a word prefix (Olive -6933)
12. Peashooters
13. Howdy Doody
14. 45 RPM records
15. S&H Green Stamps
16. Hi-fi's
17. Metal ice trays with lever
18. Mimeograph paper
19. Blue flashbulb
20. Packards
21. Roller skate keys
22. Cork popguns
23. Drive-ins
24. Studebakers
25. Wash-tub wringers

If you remembered

   0-5 = You're still young
  6-10 = You are getting older
11-15 = Don't tell your age
16-25 = You're older than dirt!

We Survived*

You lived as a child in the 1950s or the 1960s. Looking back, it's hard to believe that we have lived as long as we have.

As children, we would ride in cars with no seat belts or air bags. Riding in the back of a pickup truck on a warm day was always a special treat. Our baby cribs were covered with bright colored lead-based paint. We had no childproof lids on medicine bottles, doors or cabinets, and when we rode our bikes, we had no helmets. (Not to mention hitchhiking to town as a young kid!)

We drank water from the garden hose and not from a bottle. Horrors. We would spend hours building our go-carts out of scraps and then rode down the hill, only to find out we forgot the brakes. After running into the bushes a few times we learned to solve the problem.

We would leave home in the morning and play all day, as long as we were back when the streetlights came on. No one was able to reach us all day. No cell phones. Unthinkable. We played dodgeball and sometimes the ball would really hurt. We got cut and broke bones and broke teeth and there were no lawsuits from these accidents.

They were accidents. No one was to blame but us. Remember accidents? We had fights and punched each other and got black and blue and learned to get over it. We ate cupcakes, and bread and butter, and drank sugar soda but we were never overweight . . . we were always outside playing. We shared one grape soda with four friends, from one bottle and no one died from this?

We did not have Playstations, Nintendo 64, X Boxes, video games at all, 99 channels on cable, video tape movies, surroundsound, personal cellular phones, Personal Computers, Internet chat rooms . . . we had friends. We went outside and found them. We rode bikes or walked to a friend's home and knocked on the door, or rung the bell or just walked in and talked to them. Imagine such a thing. Without asking a parent! By ourselves! Out there in the cold cruel world! Without a guardian. How did we do it?

We made up games with sticks and tennis balls and ate worms and although we were told it would happen, we did not put out very many eyes, nor did the worms live inside us forever.

Little League had tryouts and not everyone made the team. Those who didn't had to learn to deal with disappointment . . . Some students weren't as smart as others so they failed a grade and were held back to repeat the same grade . . . Horrors. Tests were not adjusted for any reason.

Our actions were our own. Consequences were expected. No one to hide behind. The idea of a parent bailing us out if we broke a law was unheard of. They actually sided with the law, imagine that!

This generation has produced some of the best risk-takers and problem-solvers and inventors, ever. The past 50 years has been an explosion of innovation and new ideas. We had freedom, failure, success and responsibility, and we learned how to deal with it all. And you're one of them.

Congratulations

(We tried most diligently to attempt to find and credit the authors for the above sections: "Remember"; "Hey, Just How Old Are You?"; "How Many Do You Remember?"; "Older Than Dirt Quiz"; and "We Survived." However, we were unable to do so despite our best efforts. It's an endemic problem with the Internet and we wish we had the answer. — The Editors

A Bowl of Delicious Czarnina

Bob Krajewski • Class 1946 • Munster, IN

One of the ethnic food mainstays of the Polish culture is czarnina (pronounced char-nee-nah). For the uninitiated, czarnina is a delicious soup with noodles and raisins or prunes with a stock flavored with duck's blood. Sounds gross, I know, but I learned to savor it before I cared to know its ingredients. The small mom-and-pop groceries in the Harbor would sell small jars of the blood. Now the FDA would make an arrest and get them a two- to ten-year sentence.

One Christmas break while in college, a fraternity brother visited overnight, and my mother treated him to a holiday bowl of czarnina. Paul proclaimed it excellent. Being a gentleman, he didn't freak out too much when told of the ingredients.

Almost 40 years ago, our three kids were pupils at St. Stanislaus School in East Chicago, and we went to a family fun night at the gym. The food booth had a sign featuring czarnina. I asked Marge and the kids if they wanted some. They all faked gagging and throwing up.

So I walked over and asked the lady for a bowl. She grimaced and said. "Yuck! Do you eat that stuff?"
My son and his wife live in California. About a year ago, they were in Paris having a romantic anniversary dinner in a restaurant which had been in the same location for over 200 years. It overlooked the Seine River with a view of Notre Dame. For all those years it featured duck prepared in many, many ways. Tom asked about a special sauce. And the sauce? Made from duck's blood of course. "Yikes!" Tom told me he said to his wife. "I've had to travel 6,000 miles to get an exotic dinner, and I get czarnina. I could have just gone to the Harbor."

CHAPTER FOUR
4
WHS Principals and Teachers

Looking Back -Washington High School (1944-1947)

Rev. Warren Wiersbe • Class of 1947 • Lincoln, NE

I was a Depression baby (1929), so I entered the freshman class in 1944 and graduated in 1947. I thought I'd end up being a teacher, but the Good Lord had other plans and called me to be a minister and a writer. As I look back, I can see how my WHS career helped prepare me for college and seminary.

Miss Dunn taught me English grammar and Miss De-Pew helped me develop an appetite for good literature, both English and American. Our gentle librarian Ruth Lucas taught me to love books and guided me to the best ones, and I now have a library of over 10,000 volumes. Miss Brill taught me Latin and even let me teach the class when she was away because of illness. Studying Latin for two years was great preparation for the Greek and Hebrew I studied in seminary, and it also helped me better understand English grammar so I could use our marvelous language more effectively. Mr. Palmer taught me to appreciate history, and I still keep history books around to read.

Miss Swindell taught me journalism, and the experience of working on The ANVIL was valuable for a future writer and editor. I wrote the gossip column and Phil Pecar and I occasionally dropped in a "humor column" which nobody thought was funny. My years in the print shop were enriching. Mr. Altenderfer was a patient and gifted teacher.

Claude Ware, Gerald Wenzel and Andy Spencer were my successive locker partners and graciously tolerated my lack of athletic ability. I remember an extra-curricular football game in which I found myself on the line opposite Wenzel, who was built like a railway engine. The first time he blocked me, he moved every bone in my body, and that was the end of my athletic career. The coaches were tolerant and kind, but I hated gym class and swimming class, and they knew it. They tried to change me, but they were working with poor protoplasm.

Time and distance have taken me away from the Calumet Region, so I don't know where most of the "old gang" is now located; and my schedule hasn't made it possible to attend class reunions. But many school friends "rubbed off" on me in one way or another—especially Bob Krajewski, Fred Corban, John Kail and Bill Meyer. I don't know what high school students learn these days, but I can honestly give thanks for my years at "Noble Washington." I could mention many more people, but I've run out of space.

The last time we drove through East Chicago, I saw that the old buildings were gone, and I felt a twinge of regret down inside. But what my teachers and friends built into me during my high school years is still standing strong, and I wonder where I'd be today without it. I have a lot to be grateful for— thanks!

WHS Principals
1912 to 1921*   Howard H. Clark
Yearbook called "LOTUS"
1921 to 1925 T. E. Williams
Yearbook changed to "WHS SENIOR ANVIL"
1925 to 1933   Roy W.Feik
1933 to 1945   R. F. Robinson
1945 to 1956   Frank E. Cash

1956 to 1958   Dan Simon
1958 to 1963   John P. Fox
1963 to 1965   Michael Guiden
1965 to 1970   Solomon Puntillo
1970 to 1972   William Giannopoulos
1972 to 1986   Nick Ranich
*Principal contracts typically are for the period between July 1 and June
30 of the following year.*

WHS Teacher, Coach, Principal Frank E. Cash

Frank E. Cash was born into rural poverty in Boone County, Indiana. When he was seven years old his mother died. He was given up by his father to an aunt and uncle who raised him.

At Lebanon High School he was one of those natural athletes, big, strong and fast, who could play any game he put his mind to. Sports were always a part of his life. He thought it built character, discipline and teamwork, and how to handle victory and defeat. He loved history, science, English and other academic subjects.

Because he had been a good student and a good athlete, a representative from nearby Wabash College approached him with a scholarship and a job working summers in the fields on a farm or a railroad. On railroad labor gangs he worked with immigrants, many illiterate, from Ireland and eastern and southern Europe—a kind of pre-East Chicago. He saw that many of them were smart—they just hadn't had the opportunity for education.

He graduated from college in 1920 with time out for the U.S. Navy during World War I. He played football and ran track while at college. He was a starter four years and an all-Indiana (Indiana, Purdue and Notre Dame) tackle on offense and defense for two years. He also broke his nose so many times they stopped fixing it.

After college Frank worked as a substitute teacher and

assistant coach at Crawfordsville High School. His first real job in education was as a history and health teacher and coach Warsaw where he took losing programs and made the football and basketball teams among the most prominent in the state.

In 1925 he was contacted by the relatively new town of East Chicago for a teaching and coaching job. He became athletic director in 1936. In 1944 he as made principal of Washington Elementary and Columbus Schools. In 1945 he became principal at WHS. As always, he loved the students, the teachers and East Chicago. He died tragically in 1956.

"Berkowitz, Get You're A__ Out of Here!"

Harry Berkowitz, now Berke, tells a great anecdote about Frank Cash, who was a coach and/or principal for a great number of our alumni group.

Most of us saw Mr. Cash as a gruff, stern disciplinarian, and we didn't expect anything else from him.

Harry, still not a big guy, was in 1934 a small, wiry kid but nonetheless tough enough to earn a letter in football at Washington. He only earned that letter by working his butt off at practice and certainly never ever missing a practice.

One fall day in 1934, a mandatory football practice fell on a Jewish high holiday. Harry's father insisted he attend services at the temple. Harry went to his temple, but got to wondering how Coach Cash would react when he realized Harry had cut an important practice. Harry couldn't handle his dilemma easily, and after wrestling with his predicament, he finally sneaked out of the temple and dashed to football practice.

The practice had already begun, and the team was seated on the field surrounding Coach Cash, who was giving pre-drill instructions. Harry recalls there had to be about 80 players on that field; in those Depression days almost every able-bodied guy tried out for football. There wasn't too much else to do. Harry tried to sneak into an unobtrusive spot in the outermost edge of the circle when Coach Cash bellowed out, "Berkowitz, is that you?" Harry jumped up, "Yes, sir."

"Isn't today a special day for the Jewish people? Don't you belong in your temple?"

"Yes sir. I . . I . . . I just left there to get to practice," Harry stammered.

"Berkowitz, get your ass out of here! Get back to your temple as fast as you can. It's important for you to practice and show respect for your religion by attending those services. And that goes for all of you here today, whatever your religion is. Harry, we'll see you tomorrow."

Important words given at an important time in a young man's life from an unexpected source. Harry has never forgotten that incident, and it happened just a bit short of 70 years ago.

Give Thanks to Your Teachers

Tziporah Walernov (formerly Fern Goodman) •
Class of 1964 •

There are so many teachers that made an impact on my life starting at Riley Elementary and continuing on to Washington Elementary and High Schools. I'd like you to know who stands out in my mind's eye to whom I give the credit to who enabled me to communicate in a comprehensible fashion. First credit goes to my mother, Ann Evanson Goodman, class of 1937, who not only was a crafter of words and an avid cross-word-puzzle solver, but also an indefatigable golden storybook reader, she gave me the base vocabulary on which I attached all the other learning from my teacher's lessons. She must have read the Pokey Little Puppy to me 100 times or more, not to mention the King Solomon stories, etc. Here are teachers who strongly impacted my future career achievements as a journalism teacher, a creative writing teacher, an English comp teacher, a listening skills teacher and a TESL teacher:

Miss Sheldon, Miss Hayes, Miss Rae Johnson, Mrs. Sutton and Mr. Hughes.

Do you remember them? Here are some thumbnail sketches to act as memory joggers. Miss Sheldon was a petite woman with salt and pepper short hair. Her focus was on teaching us to dissect sentences. It often felt as if she were calling me to dissect my inner workings or pull out some skill I wasn't sure I had within me. Day after day, she called us to the board multiple times to dissect sentences with adverbial clauses, prepositional phrases, nouns and predicates. She also expected us to have a broad comprehension and mature reasoning ability. She did not accept rote learning as worthy of us as individuals. She respected our innate ability to have meaningful dialogue and analysis of books and articles. She was the first to treat me and my classmates like people—not puppets.

Remember Miss Hayes with her purple hair and tapping ruler on our desks? She scared us into learning a huge volume of information. It seems all students hated to be in her classroom, while at the same time respecting all she was able to accomplish, and most people I know felt she was responsible for making us the success we became in higher grades. I remember reciting aloud, "A noun is the name of a person, place or thing" daily, both individually in answer to a question and as a group to start the day. We memorized definitions for all the parts of speech. We also had very precisely aligned margins in her class and if we didn't have it right, we could count on that ruler coming down hard on our desk. She was Roumanian and so was my Grandma, and sometimes we'd talk about liking mommilega after the school bell rang and the class was dismissed. She died of leukemia and it was a great loss to our community. I believe she also required us to memorize short verses which she would ask us to stand behind our desk and recite alone, "I shot an arrow into the air, where it landed I knew not where."

In High School, Johnny Sutton greatly expanded our

world by bringing in speakers from far-flung places with inspirational stories of high intrigue and adventure like the Von Trapp Family before the "Sound of Music" was on the drawing board, and a man from Lebanon who wrote the book, a "Syrian Yankee." She taught us in Assembly the corrected version of the Pledge of Allegiance where the comma had been removed after nation, in one nation under God. Today, 40+ years later, people still do it wrong, but none of us who learned from Johnny Sutton do it wrong. Her drama classes helped us take Shakespeare and other writing and made it come alive through intonation and expression. She taught us how to "dress-up" our talents in the Spring Follies and fall talent show. We girls got the chance to be models for Butterick and Simplicity . . . pretty heady stuff!

Mr. Hughes ran the debate teams and the SENATORIAL news. He put us in the context where polished products were expected and we rose to the challenge. He suggested I read Carlos Castenedas, something more adult-like and philosophical than I would have chosen had I been left to my own selection process. Last, but not least, was Rae Johnson who had an amaryllis plant that literally rose in height overnight. She kept it on her desk and we witnessed its emergence as a rite of spring and of a sophomore English class. We memorized "Ode to a Lark," "Daffodils," "What a tangled web we weave when we first endeavor to deceive," "Forever and forever and forever creeps on this petty pace from day to day to the last syllable of recorded time," from Shakespeare. We read "A Tale of Two Cities" by Dickens and found out what Cliff's Notes were all about. Now you are probably thinking the only part that stuck was the "forever and forever" part, judging from the length of this, but there was one other phrase that stuck too: "All good things must come to an end." Write back with your remembrances and any updated info you may have. With that I bid you all adieu.

From an Original Anvil Assistant Editor

Mary Ann Thornburg • Class of 1950 • Rincon, GA

I enjoy reading the ANVIL. I even recognized a few names. I graduated in 1950 and remember being assistant editor of the ANVIL in 1948 or 1949. At that time, we were all in Mr. Kincaid's printing class. Not only did we write and set up the paper—we had a wonderful time with Mr. Kincaid and Mr. Matovich. I also remember Hanak's Bakery—great memories and great pastries.

I wish you and the ANVIL staff good luck in your endeavors—keeping the memories alive.

Meeting with Carl (Pinky) Johnson

Michael Arsulich • Class of 1946 • San Diego, CA

About three years ago (circa 1997), I flew to Chicago to see the Notre Dame-USC football game at South Bend. Gerald Wenzell, class of 1947, told me that Pinky Johnson, our chemistry professor, was still living in DeMotte. I called him well ahead of time to arrange a meeting with him and his wife. Having had so many students in his day, I don't think he remembered me. He was 91 at the time. I told him the years that I attended Washington High. He told me about some of the school politics that were going on during 1943-1946. Wow! It was enlightening indeed.

I took him out to lunch at a restaurant just north of town on the edge of the Kankakee River. Fish is their specialty.

Before I departed, I took about two minutes of film of him with my cassette-inserted handi-cam. I think I still have it somewhere. He gave me two ANVILs as a momento. I noticed they were signed by him. I noticed in one of your monthly's

60

that his name was mentioned. He was more than that! He was a graduate valedictorian of East Chicago High in 1922. He enrolled as a freshman at the University of Illinois. Upon completion of his studies, he joined the East Chicago School System in some junior high school. In his chemistry classes, his course of study in chemistry was interesting as well as meaningful.

He dedicated himself to the youth of East Chicago. He was helpful to the athletic coaches by scouting next week's opponent. During the summers, he managed Camp Wright Boy Scout Camp near Rochester, Indiana. I was there in the summer of 1941. It gave us a chance to escape the smoke, soot, dust, iron dust and chemical substances that polluted the air. He could have gone to school or taken a vacation. If that wasn't dedication to us kids, show me another example. Frank [Hanak], you and I were enrolled in Mrs. Winner's speech class at E.C.I.U. Extension in the fall of 1947. USC beat Notre Dame that year. I belong to San Diego's Trojan Club, having earned a master's there a number of years ago. Keep up the good work.

How About These Teachers?

Paul and Jeanette Bramer • Classes of 1958 & 1956 • East Chicago, IN

Remember Mamie Overpeck and Florence Johnson, our math teachers? Or Ray Krajewski, where I learned German? How about Miss White, a very calm lady? Pete Pinsack who said, "Necessity is the mother of invention" and so many more.

My wife, Jeanette Vendramin, class of 1956, and I walked all over the Harbor. Go to the movies and whatever, no problems. We would go to Skretny's, if he didn't have it, you didn't need it. We miss them.

Match 'Em Up
Bob Krajewski • Class of 1946 • Munster, IN

One of the staples of many high school newspapers or yearbooks is a listing of the categorical best or top ten. We have all seen some of those lists: cutest girl, handsomest boy, best smile, friendliest, and on and on. When I worked on the Weekly and SENIOR ANVILs, I suggested a similar treatment of our teachers, but alas, censorship was unrelenting in those days. So, I'm finally able, fifty-five years later, to offer a matching quiz of personal characteristics with WHS teachers. There are, however, no right or wrong answers to this quiz.

Okay, you can argue with both sides of this match-up quiz. Some may question the omission of a favorite teacher or one most despised; some might have included other personal characteristics. To those critics, I can only say, I had fun making this one; you can make up one listing only those teachers you encountered. Of course, one's ratings are a function of one's personal contacts. If you didn't take Latin, you probably never had Miss Brill.

What I, and I believe what most alums, would be interested in is who would be the best all-around teacher from each decade. So, all are encouraged to write us and tell us who you rate as the best teacher you ever had at WHS. Give us an anecdote or two about that teacher to illustrate your opinion. We will all appreciate your efforts.

The teachers listed are representative (from my perspective) of those who taught during the years the majority of our alumni group attended. I've omitted "best" and "worst" when their use is understood.

Match the teacher with the description you see fits best to your experience. Compare your choices with friends and family! It's fun!

Teacher	Description
John Baratto	affected
Floyd Bolton	animated
George Boniecki	authoritative
Nick Brunswick	autocratic
Miss Dunn	bizarre
Miss Flinn	boring
Mr. Foster	caring
Miss Gabor	dashing
Sam Geddes	deadpan
Bill Giannopouos	best disciplinarian
Mike Guiden	worst disciplinarian
Paul Guiden	easiest grader
Jim Hughes	toughest grader
Miss Kozacik	eccentric
Ray Krajewski	friendliest
Hobart Lidster	funniest
Eli Matovich	handsomest
Miss Mendenhall	helpful
Bemhardt Mintz	interesting
Walter McCoy	kindest
Miss McDonald	prettiest
Miss Oilar	smartest
Don PaHa	best smile
Charles Palmer	best dressed
Jim Porter	sourest
Sol Puntillo	weirdest
Homer Reeves	all around best teacher
Mr. Souter	strictest
Miss Sowerby	most lenient
Nick Young	oldest

Harlan Walley	youngest
Sam Weinstein	sporty
John Zitko	gruffest

Teacher's Nicknames

Ron Lax • Class of 1949 • Mesa, AZ

Mr. Altenderfer	TV
Mr. Geddes	Sammy
Mr. Johnson	Pinky
Miss McIntosh	Tiny
Miss Skrentny	Stasha
Mr. Reeves	Buckshot
Mr. Robinson	Big Bob

From the April 11, 1945, Weekly ANVIL

Some Memories of WHS Math

John Maniotes • Class of 1953 • Munster, IN

Although many of the memories and recollections of WHS High School center on our great athletic teams, few of the alumni ever mention some of the great academic programs at WHS. My recollections have always included the excellent WHS math teachers that I had starting with my freshman year (1949) through my senior year (1953).

Who could forget such great math teachers as:

Miss Florence Johnson

Miss Jessie Mendenhall

Miss Mamie Overpeck

Mr. Clyde Kellam

I had these teachers for introductory, intermediate and advanced plane and solid geometry and trigonometry. If you were in the "college prep" program, these courses were required, and they involved a lot of work.

There was no "spoon feeding" of mathematics by these teachers to the students. I remember doing the "drill and practice" math problems in class on the blackboard or on paper, and I remember that we always had homework to do in the evening. The teachers were "tough" but fair in grading our homework, quizzes and exams. It was good to learn from your own mistakes, but it was also better to learn from the mistakes of others when the solutions to the math problems were discussed in class. After all, as Mr. Kellam would say: "Isn't education itself a process of learning, not only from your mistakes, but from the mistakes of others."

Miss Overpeck always encouraged us to do extra credit algebra problems and hand them in the next day. Those problems she assigned were always challenging and it was difficult to get a perfect score.

When I was studying geometry and trigonometry, I was overwhelmed by the concept of doing "proofs." How could anyone progress unerringly along a logical path using theorems, lemmas and corollaries to solve a "proof"? It was always a great relief when Miss Johnson and Miss Mendenhall explained clearly the solution to a "proof." They further told us it was quite common for students to make many false starts and come to many deadends before arriving upon the solution.

Who can forget the complex "word problems" that we had to read and solve in our algebra, geometry and trigonometry classes. All of these math teachers had us apply the "divide and conquer" technique to solve these large complex problems. That is, you took the original difficult problem and broke it into smaller and more manageable sub-problems, each of which was easier to solve than the original problem. We were expected to divide each of the difficulties into as many parts as possible, and to think in an orderly fashion, beginning with those matters which are simplest and easiest to understand and working toward those which are more complex.

During my years at Purdue University, I encountered complex "word problems" again throughout my math, physics, chemistry and engineering courses. These problems were extremely abstract and difficult to visualize. Fortunately, by using the "divide and conquer" technique that the WHS math teachers taught me, I was well prepared to solve these problems.

The WHS math teachers will always be ranked among the best. They served as role models throughout my own career. The basic concepts that they taught me prepared me for working toward and obtaining B.S., M.S. and PhD. degrees in Engineering at Purdue University.

The math teachers were always well prepared for class and they took the time to work with their students. They had the ability to bring interest and excitement to even the most tedious aspects of their math classes. The values they also taught us were discipline, work and time management. If you followed these principles, you could succeed in any task you set out to do.

After 38 years of teaching at Purdue University Calumet, I retired in May 2001, as Professor, Information Systems and Computer Programming, there is not a day that goes by that I don't apply some of the math skills that I acquired from the ECW math teachers.

Miss Aldrin's Ethnic Days

Josephine Grdinich Mosca • Class of 1941 • Highland, IN

The Harbor side of East Chicago was unique with its own league of nationalities. Does anyone remember Miss Eleanor Aldrin, auditorium teacher at Riley School? She encouraged us to be proud of our heritage. I believe it was May 18, "Good-Will Day," every year that she had us participate in a program on stage in costumes of our nationalities and do the different dances—it was so much fun practicing for the program. Booths were set up in the gym for each nationality and do so we could learn about others.

Being of Croatian descent, we did the Kolo dances. How many still remember this from the 1930s? I can still picture the Mihalareas brothers (Nick and John) in their Greek costumes.

Thanks to the ANVIL for helping us relive the memories of our school days.

Teachers Resemble Favorite Comic Heroes!
(A column from the ANVIL, Oct. 26, 1949)

Blondie—Miss Murphy
Tille the Toiler—MissSufana
Mutt and Jeff—Mr. Parker and Mr. Saboff
Superman—Mr. Frieberger
Ferd'nand—Mr. Kincaid
Smiling Jack—Mr. Recenberger
Terry and the Pirates—Mr. Altenderfer and
    the Washington Brothers
Popeye the Sailor—Mr. Lidster
Buck Rogers—Mr. Johnson
Joe Palooka—Mr. Geddes
Brenda Starr—Miss Skrentny

Mr. Kellam

Ronald Lax • Class of 1949 • Mesa, AZ

How many of you took a mathematics class with Mr. Kellam? Remember, Mr. Kellam was the dean of boys and also taught trigonometry. I really liked Mr. Kellam and enjoyed his class. I thought he was a perfect gentleman. He reminded me of my dad. Years later, when I was a public school teacher of mathematics for over 25 years, I tried to pattern my teaching methods to be like Mr. Kellam. (I also remember Miss Sharp and Miss Mendenhall as being fine teachers.) We had a great faculty at WHS.

Orchestra Teacher

Kathleen Main Sweeney • Class of 1945 • Highland, N

I would like to add Edward Tritt to the list of teachers to be recognized in the WHS book. Mr. Tritt was the orchestra teacher and my private violin teacher all through my years at Washington. I graduated in 1945 and because of his encouragement and willingness to go the extra mile for me, I was able to attend DePauw University the following fall. He helped prepare me for an audition for a scholarship and even wrote a letter to the Dean of the Music School on my behalf. Thanks to him, I was awarded a scholarship and four years later received a bachelor's degree in music. Attending DePauw would not have been a possibility for me if it hadn't been for Mr. Tritt's expert teaching ability and his help.

Mr. Tritt left East Chicago and moved his family to California soon after 1945 to teach at the University of Redlands. I had no further contact with him after graduation, but have always remembered and appreciated what he did for me.

From the Harbor to the Present

Bill Giannopoulos • Class of 1942 • Cape Coral, FL

The cycle is complete, the 18-year-old lad to the 76-year-old in his golden Greek years. You can take the boy out of "Da Harbor," not "Da Harbor" out of the boy.

Hershel Cook called me and informed me about the ECWAA and forwarded 20-30 past issues of the ANVIL. Reading the articles made me feel young again. It reminded me that some of the best years of my life were at good old WHS.

It is amazing how quickly memories were awakened after reading the ANVIL issues. The class of 1942 certainly proved that the Harbor was a melting pot of our nation. 1912 produced the most Grecian graduates (20) in any one graduating class.

The articles in the ANVIL reminded me of all my boyish crushes/puppy loves; Virginia Chustoff, Rose Dezamko, Sophie Gorman, Marjorie Haskett, Betty Jean Halem, Connie Kyriakos, Marjorie Lausen, Olga McKenzie, Pat Petzer, Betty Jane Rosenberry, Juanita Timmerman, Eileen Williams, Evelyn Patchman, and I'm sure I had ten underclassmen like Betty Garner and Shirley Toff on my mind.

You will notice that Kathryn Korentoures is not listed under crushes in my life. She became the love of my life during the War years, 1943-1945. After 56 married years, our union has produced three children, seven grandchildren, and two great grandchildren. Please know that I will be an article contributor to the ANVIL as often as your editor will permit. Such titles as "How the Senior Class Presidency was Won," School years-student, teacher, principal," "Dime a Dance," etc, will follow.

Jake Arzumanian and Reserved Parking

Bob Krajewski • Class of 1946 • Munster, IN

Reading about Jake Arzumanian's recent induction into the Indiana Baseball Coaches Hall of Fame led me to recall an almost forgotten incident that domonstrated the impact of some of the personalities of the Harbor.

During the wind-up of the 1985 high school basketball tourney, I was the acting State Superintendent of Public Instruction. I was on temporary leave from EC Schools and had the position for only a short time until the governor appointed a full-time replacement for the elected official who had resigned suddenly. The semi-state tourney at Purdue was a kind of official duty call for the State Superintendent, and the Indiana High School Athletic Association sent along, of course, complimentary tickets, However, they overlooked the perk of a spot in the reserved parking lot just steps away from the doors to the gym.

If you've ever been to Purdue for football or basketball games, you're aware of what a hassle parking can become.

Even though I didn't have a parking pass, I hoped my Harbor refined bluster and my official position and official car would get me into the preferred lot. And that official car was the biggest Buick of that era with a license plate that read something like "Indiana State" with a big star in the middle and a number six.

My approach to the minor bureaucrat in charge of the parking lot was to no avail. He told me that he was ordered to allow no one in, no matter who, if they didn't have the proper pass. It was really no big deal for me, so I moved along.

During the break between games, I was taking a walk to the concession stands when I ran into Jake Arzumanian. We were old friends over thirty years, and we greeted each other heartily. He invited me into the tournament director's office and Jake introduced me to the gang there.

We chatted about basketball and the upcoming state budget for education, and then I humorously needled the tourney director about my parking situation. I said, "here I am, the number one public school official in the State of Indiana, technically the overseer of a million students, the educational leader of almost one hundred thousand professionals, responsible for an annual budget of over two billion dollars annually, and I can't get in your parking lot!"

"Bob," he replied, "why didn't you tell us you knew Jake Arzumanian? We'd have gotten you right in there!"

There are certainly several lessons in this context, and I've enjoyed retelling that anecdote to demonstrate that one shouldn't be too full of oneself. It demonstrates the camaraderie of athletes and coaches everywhere, and sometimes insular world they live in, but, most of all, it demonstrates that Jake Arzumanian was and is appreciated and respected across the state of Indiana.

Educators to the Power of 17

Bill Giannopoulos • Class of 1942 • Cape Coral, FL

I know teacher's salaries are low and teaching is tougher now than in prior years. There were no distractions, such as TV, CD players, cell phones and personal autos. The student walked and/or ran back and forth to home for lunch. No one even heard of free breakfast and lunches. So, why is it that so many of the class of 1942 became educators? Was it that parents really took an interest and instilled in one's child that to get ahead one needed an education? Seventeen of the class of 1942 went into education and taught and/or became administrators in the E.C. Public Schools or neighboring districts. My first position in 1950 after graduating from Indiana University was teaching mathematics in Charlestown, Indiana, for the sum of $2500 per year. The following year, I was offered $2850 in New Albany, Indiana, but I could not pass up the offer of $3500 from the E.C.P.S. in 1951. Wow! Teaching in my hometown was one of life's real pleasures and ambitions. I stayed in the E.C.P.S. for 16 years and retired in 1987. The following 17 classmates went into the same profession:

Secondary level:
Ed Baran, Principal RHS
Paul Barkal, RHS
Bill Giannopoulos, Supervisor of Mathematics and Principal
Irene Mamnik, Supervisor of Health Services
Elaine Chovanec, School Nurse
Eugene Martin, Supervisor of Language Arts
Matthew Racich, WHS
Frank Sufak, WHS
Francis Sutkowski, WHS
Rudy Voica, WHS
Tom Faulkner, WHS
Elementary/Junior High School Level:
Kathryn Fields, Principal Gosch, Field
Walter Matusik, Principal Gosch, Block Junior H.S.
Other Schools:
James Faulkner, Whiting H.S.
John Michelareas, Hammond Schools
School Board Members:
John Suty
Salvatore Nunez

We do thank all our teachers for lessons well learned and our parents for instilling in us that education is the first step to success. I am proud to say that at one time or another, I served with each of my classmates in the E.C.P.S.

Mildred Johnston Sutton, My Mentor

Natalie Stepanovich Vujovich • Class of 1949 • Munster, IN

There is no doubt that the teacher who most influenced me was Mildred Johnston Sutton. My first contact with Miss Johnston was at Washington Elementary, in a class we called "Auditorium" where we read aloud poetry and performed children's plays. She had a Master's Degree from Northwestern University and had traveled the world, and I loved listening to her tell of her experiences. She exposed us to the best in literature, from Longfellow's "Hiawatha" to the Biblical Psalms. In class she was a strict disciplinarian and took no nonsense from anyone. Outside of class she was the leader of my Girl Scout Troop and helped us earn badges and led us on some fun adventures.

Mildred Johnston Sutton

Shortly after I finished junior high school, Miss Johnston joined the WHS faculty where she taught drama and literature. In her class we put on abridged performances of such classic plays, as Shakespeare's "Taming of the Shrew" and Chekov's "The Marriage Proposal." Outside of class she directed popular modern all-school productions such as "A Date With Judy," "You Can't Take It With You," and "Brewster's Millions." We learned to work as stage crew and what went on behind the curtain. She organized field trips to take us to see plays.

As a sponsor of the National Forensic League, Miss Johnston helped me to prepare a dramatic interpretation from "Medea" that took me to semi-state competition. In the summer between my junior and senior years in high school, she encouraged me to attend the National High School Institute at

Northwestern University's School of Speech. This proved to be such a worthwhile experience that later my younger brother David and my sister Dawn also attended the same program. I am sure that Miss Johnston's recommendation was influential in my receiving the Indiana Vassar Club Scholarship in 1949. It was during my freshman year at Vassar that Indiana withdrew the requirement that female teachers be unmarried. She then became Mrs. Herbert Sutton.

As the years passed, I never lost contact with "Johnnie," as she was familiarly called. After my marriage to George Radich and raising our daughters to school age, I followed in her footsteps and began to teach English and Speech at WHS in 1967. This was a short time before her retirement, so she was there to turn to for advice. It was the beginning of my nineteen years of teaching at Washington and two years at E.C. Central that I will always treasure.

Mildred Johnston Sutton is now 96 years old and lives in a retirement home in Florida where I have visited her. I will forever be indebted to her for the exposure to the arts and the love and inspiration she gave me.

CHAPTER FIVE
5
Heroes and Special Achievers

Emilio Albert De La Garza, Jr., Class of 1968
By: Narcissa Castillo • Class of 1947 • Munster, IN

Emilio Albert De La Garza, Jr., was born June 21, 1949, in East Chicago, Indiana. He graduated from Washington High School in East Chicago in 1968. For a year he worked at Inland Steel Company in East Chicago.

On February 4, 1969, he enlisted in the U.S. Marines in Chicago, Illinois. He was transferred to the Marine Corps Recruit Depot, San Diego, California, where he received Recruit training with the 2nd Recruit Training Battalion. Upon completion of recruit training, he was ordered to the Marine Corps Base, Camp Pendleton, California, where he joined the 2nd Infantry Training Regiment and underwent individual combat training with the 1st and 2nd Battalions, and weapons training with the Basic Infantry Training Battalion.

Medal of Honor recipient, Emilio Albert De La Garza, Jr.

On July 1, 1969, he was promoted to private first class. On July 25, 1969, he arrived in the Republic of Vietnam for duty as Ammo Carrier, Company "II' 2nd Battalion, 3rd

Marine Division (Rein). On September 29, 1969, he was reassigned to the 1st Marine Division and served as a Marine Corps Exchange man with Headquarters and Service Company, 2nd Battalion, 1st Marines, until the following December. On February 1, 1970, he was promoted to lance corporal.

Corporal De La Garza then joined Company "B," 2nd Battalion, 1st Marines, 1st Marine Division. With one month remaining to serve in Vietnam while serving as a machine gunner on squad-size patrol with the 3rd Platoon of Company "E," about four miles south of Da Nang on April 11, 1970, he was mortally wounded.

His medals and decorations include: the Purple Heart, the Combat Action Ribbon, the National Defense Service Metal, the Vietnam Service Metal with one bronze star and the Republic of Vietnam Campaign Medal.

In 1971, Vice President Spiro T. Agnew presented his parents with the Medal of Honor in Washington.

He was survived by his wife Rosemary, who is now remarried, and daughter Renee, his parents, Mr. and Mrs. Emilio and Carmen De La Garza, Sr., and one brother, Guadalupe Lee. Mr. Emilio D La Garza, Sr. is a World War II veteran and Guadalupe Lee is a veteran of the Marines.

De La Garza was the only recipient of the nation's highest honor for bravery among the more than 16,000 people from Lake County who served in Vietnam. He was one of only two people from all of Indiana to win the award for service during the war. He was a volunteer to go to Vietnam. He was a volunteer the night he was killed.

In 1973, a new American Legion unit—Post 508, in East Chicago was named for De La Garza. In 1981, an $11 million vocational center on Columbus Drive also was named in honor of the 1968 graduate of East Chicago Washington High School.

Ivy Tech State College took over the operation of the

De La Garza Career Center and has added a wall panel in the college's lobby with a bronze bust of De La Garza as a backdrop.

There is also a street in Oceanside, California, near the Marine base there that bears De La Garza's name. The Medal of Honor is the highest award for bravery that can be given to any individual in the United States.

The deed must be proved by incontestable evidence at least two eyewitnesses; it must be so outstanding that it clearly distinguishes the recipient's gallantry beyond the call of duty from lesser forms of bravery; it must involve the risk of his/her life; and it must be the type of deed which, if he/she had not done it, would not subject him/her in any justified criticism.

The idea for the Medal of Honor was born during the Civil War as men fought gallantly and oftentimes displayed great heroism. George Washington originated the Purple Heart in 1782 to honor brave soldiers, sailors and marines. From that time until the Civil War, Certificates of Merit and a "brevet" system of promotion were used as military awards. The first military decoration formally authorized by the American Government as a badge of valor was the Medal of Honor for enlisted men of the Navy and Marine Corps. It was authorized by Congress, and approved by President Abraham Lincoln on December 21, 1861. The medal for the Army and Voluntary Forces was authorized on July 12, 1862.

The medal is awarded "in the name of the Congress of the United States," and for this reason, it is often called the Congressional Medal of Honor. It is only on rare occasions, however, that Congress awards special Medals of Honor. An Executive Order, signed by President Theodore Roosevelt on September 20, 1905, directed that ceremonies of award "will always be made with formal and impressive ceremonial," and that the recipient "will, when practicable, be ordered to Washington, DC, and the presentation will be made by the

President, as Commander in Chief; or by such representative as the President may designate."

The Navy Medal of Honor is made of bronze, suspended by an anchor from a bright blue ribbon, and is worn about the neck. The ribbon is spangled with a cluster of 13 white stars representing the original States. Each ray of the five pointed star contains sprays of laurel and oak and is tipped with a trefoil. Standing in bas-relief circled by 34 stars representing the 34 States in 1861, is Minerva, who personifies the Union. She holds in her left hand the fasces, an ax bound in staves of wood, which is the ancient Roman symbol of authority. With the shield in her right hand, she repulses the serpents held by the crouching figure of Discord. The reverse of the medal is left blank, allowing for the engraving of the recipient's name and the date and place of his deed.

Medal of Honor

MARINE LANCE CORPORAL EMILIO A. DE LA GARZA, JR., EAST CHICAGO

The Medal of Honor Citation:

"For conspicuous gallantry and intrepidity at the risk of his life above and beyond the call of duty while serving as a machine gunner with Company E, Second Battalion, First Marines, First Marine Division, in the Republic of Vietnam on April 1, 1970."

"Returning with his squad from a night ambush operation, Lance Corporal De La Garza joined his platoon commander and another Marine in searching for the enemy soldiers who had been observed fleeing for cover toward a small pond. Moments later, he located one of the enemy soldiers hiding among the reeds and brush."

"As the three Marines attempted to remove the resisting soldier from the pond, Lance Corporal De La Garza observed him pull the pin on a grenade. Shouting a warning, Lance Corporal De La Garza placed himself between the other two Marines and the ensuing blast from the grenade, thereby saving the lives of his comrades at the sacrifice of his own."

Vincent Boryla • Class of 1944

Basketball All-American–Participant in 1948 London Olympics
By: Archibald McKinlay • Class of 1945 • Chicago, IL— From "The Times," Sunday, August 2, 1992

Calumet Roots

In this Olympic season, when the world seems agog at the basketball "dream team," let us recall the only Regionite ever to win a gold for basketball. Vince Boryla was not only an olympian in the athletic sense, but, as his subsequent career demonstrated, in the same sense of being like an olympian god, exalted and majestic, if not celestial. He even lives on a mountain. He was and is the embodiment of the Amercian dream, the perfect model for young people with talent wondering how to best invest it.

Vincent Boryla

Like a classic American hero, Vinny began humbly. The son of Polish immigrants, Vinny grew up in Indiana Harbor, an awkward, somewhat outsized boy. When running all out, the sound of his plodding footsteps preceded him by a city block. He was the only kid in his gang with a negative vertical leap. In the children's game of rubbing the stomach while patting the head, he alternately wore himself bald and knocked himself out. At

79

kick-the-can, he was the only kid who needed a holder. As for hopscotch, he was twice blamed for seismograph blips in California.

But, Vinny's revenge was that he had brains galore parlayed with a persistent streak that made Horatio Alger seem like Rip Van Winkle. Gradually, he improved his foot-speed, spring, coordination and other skills, until he at last became not only proficient at competition but Bunyaneque. He could shoot baskets with the accuracy normally associated with jack-lightning Harborites picking off rats at the city dump. He could hit a bushel basket with a football spiraled more than sixty yards in the air. And there are people still around who swear that the softballs he hit with Excalibur-the-bat preceded Sputnik into orbit by more than two decades.

By the end of his senior year at Washington High, Vinny was the uncrowned best basketball player in Indiana. And, at Notre Dame, surrounded by the best of the best, he quickly became a starter and an All-American as a freshman, breaking the school's scoring record. Like a proper hero, he modestly credits his success to Doc Irwin, his coach as a senior at WHS (1944) and a man who did not merely manage players, but tutored them.

"Doc knew more basketball than all other coaches I ever played under, high school, college, service, AAU or pro," Vinny once said. "He was fundamentally light years ahead of them all. He just knew the game."

After his freshman year, Vinny was drafted and went into the Navy, and after boot camp, entered the Naval Academy. When World War II hostilities ended, Vinny asked to be released from the Academy so that he could return to his pre medical school studies at Notre Dame. After playing a second year with the Irish, and about to be drafted a second time (the war not "officially" over), he enlisted in the army and played for a Fort Sheridan team that, largely because of his presence, became one of the finest service teams in the nation.

Transferred to Fort Lowry, he played the next season for the post team as well as for the AAU Denver Nuggets, from which he was picked to play in the 1948 Olympics in London. After the service, he transferred to the University of Denver, again made All-American, and after one year, turned pro with the New York Knickerbockers. After playing five years and making the NBA All Star Team three times, he coached the Knicks for two years, then became general manager and was associated with the Knicks for ten years. He later had an interest in the Utah Stars and was president and general manager of the professional Denver Nuggets, in which capacity he was named NBA executive of the year.

No man ever excelled on more levels of basketball, which is Olympian in itself. Vinny applied himself to the books as much as to the hardwood. And, he took advantage of opportunities, for example, his games in Madison Square Garden. As a freshman, he scored 26 points there, as a sophomore he had another 20-point game, during the Olympic Trials in 1948, he scored 35 points, and as a University of Denver hook-shot phenom, he scored 36 against St. John's. This led to a long-term relationship with Ned Irish, impresario of Madison Square Garden and the New York Knicks.

While with the Knicks, Vinny worked the off-season unloading merchandise at an A & P warehouse on Long Island and later operating a day camp in Denver. By the time he headed west, he had a wife, two children and $75,000. This became principal that he guarded zealously, never cutting into it. He then used that principal to go into a real estate partnership with the second owner of the Nuggets. (Jay Ambrose, the first owner of the AAU Nuggets had also been Vinny's mentor.) They bought farm land surrounding Denver, sat on it, and sold parreceiving tributes from one's subjects. (He still owns an interest in 30 acres.)

Vinny got to where he could make a million as easily as most people make breakfast. A few years ago, for examples of it during suburbamania, which was like being king and, he bought a drive-in movie, a mile-and-an-eighth from the airport in Denver, anticipating a sale to a group of parking lot moguls. When the moguls backed out of the deal, patient Vinny operated the drive-in until the moguls had a second change of heart. Naturally, he negotiated a much better deal than before. He ended up with a million-dollar profit and another million-and-a-half profit for his partners.

Interesting, Vinny never sought anything, just worked hard and did whatever had to be done. As to the secret of his success, Vinny said: "I never BSed myself or anyone else." Well, Vinny, you're half right.

[FOOTNOTE: Vince Boryla won an Olympic gold medal in 1948, only the second time basketball was an Olympic sport. The only previous time basketball was played as an Olympic sport was in 1936. However, it was a demonstration sport in 1904.]

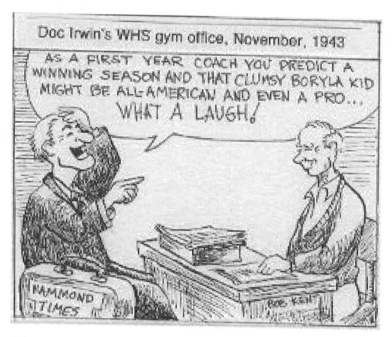

Honorable Lorenzo Arredondo • Class of 1960

Judge Arredondo is in his twenty-third (23) year as a trial judge. He has been a member of the faculty of the National Judicial College and the Indiana Judicial Conference and the Board of Managers of the Indiana Judges Association. He is Past Chair of the Commission on Opportunities for Minorities in the Profession of the Indiana State Bar Association and has served as Chair of the Improvements in the Courts Committee of the Indiana State Bar Association. Also, he is the Past Chair of the American Bar Association Task Force of the Judicial Administration Division, on Opportunities in the Judiciary and served on the Executive Committee of the Conference of State Trial Judges. He is on the Board of Directors of the American Judicature Society, the Indiana State Bar Association, and the Indiana Equal Justice Fund. He is the recipient of the Sherman Minton Judicial Excellence Award and the Rabb Emison Achievement Award.

Honorable
Lorenzo Arredondo

In 1983, Judge Arredondo was elected President of the National Hispanic Bar Association. He has served as Chair of the National Hispanic Bar Association's Judicial Council and is a member of its founders circle.

Locally, Judge Arredondo is a life member of the Latino Historical Society of Northwest Indiana. He is a member of the National Association of Latino Elected Officials and is included among the "Who's Who of Hispanic Americans." Now he is a member of the WHS Alumni Association.

Alex Vraciu, Jr. • Class of 1937

By: Archibald McKinlay • Class of 1945 • Chicago, IL

There was nothing in his background that suggested he would become the Red Baron of the Navy. Delivered by a midwife at home in Indiana Harbor, this handsome son of a Romanian hotelkeeper and policeman was was simply a well mannered, good student inclined toward aesthetics and enjoyment of the fine things in life. It surprised no one in his Block-Pennsy neighborhood, therefore, when following graduation from Washington High School in 1937, Alex Vraciu, Jr. won an academic scholarship to DePauw University.

But, the war was coming and when the government offered Civilian Pilot Training (CPI), Alex took advantage of it between his junior and senior years in college, and following graduation in 1941, just prior to Pearl Harbor, he entered naval flight training. After earning his wings in August, 1942, and qualifying for carriers in Lake Michigan on a converted excursion ship, he became wingman for Lieutenant Commander Edward H. (Butch) O'Hare, the Medal of Honor winner for whom O'Hare Airport is named. While flying section lead in October, 1943, at Wake Island, Alex shot down his first enemy aircraft, a Japanese Zero. He next got a bomber at Tarawa, and on January 29, 1944, he became an "Ace" after downing three more bombers over Kwajalein, the last destroyed after a long, low-level pursuit with only one gun firing part-time.

At the first Truk raid, February 16, he notched three Zeros and one Rufe in a wild dogfight, but lost his carrier, the Intrepid, which was torpedoed.

Sent Stateside, Alex asked to be returned to combat duty, and the Navy assigned him to the Lexington. He downed two more Zeroes at the second Truk raid on April 29, and shot down another bomber, his 12th kill, north of Saipan on June 12th. By then, he was seeking out fat-bellied Betty bombers because he had been told it was one of them that had shot down Butch O'Hare. Vraciu next (on June 14) sank a large enemy merchant ship, with a direct hit on its stern. And then, on June 19, he experienced his most productive time in the Navy. Within just eight minutes, Alex Vraciu bagged six dive-bombers! Working in close because of his oil-streaked windshield, he incredibly used only 360 rounds of ammunition. The next day, while flying escort for bomber and torpedo planes on a record, long-range strike against the Japanese fleet in the First Philippine Sea battle, he shot down a Zero, and damaged another. At that point, he was America's leading Naval Ace.

Naturally, the Navy sent him home to sell war bonds. He hated it, but it did have its moments. More than 6,000 townspeople greeted him at a homecoming ceremony at Block Stadium. Mayor Frank Migas, Governor Henry F. Schricker, and many others sang his praises. It was during this visit home that he met and married the prettiest girl in town, 21-year-old Kathryn Horn, who in high school had been the perennial Miss Washington. Vraciu then returned to the Pacific, but he had used up all his luck. While strafing near Clark Field in the Philippines on December 14, anti-aircraft fire shot him down, and after sticking with the plane long enough to avoid winding up on the enemy airfield, he parachuted into a clearing in the jungle where guerrillas met him and put him in charge of 180, men. Hearing that McArthur would soon land, he led the group toward a link-up. On the way, however, they were suddenly ambushed by another band of guerillas, it turned out, and the three men next to him were shot and killed. Finally, though Alex Vraciu, Jr. of Indiana Harbor marched into an American camp sporting a Japanese pistol, a Japanese sword, and an inch-long beard.

For his exploits, Vraciu was honored by the East Chicago Hall of Fame on April 26, 1987, at the K.C. Hall. In all, Vraciu shot down 19 planes, destroyed 21 more on the ground, and survived service on six carriers (two of which were torpedoed), two ditchings, and two parachute jumps, as he became known as both The Indestructible and Grumman Aircraft's best customer.

Twelve years after the war, jet test pilot Vraciu showed he still was the best when he won the High Individual Air-to-Air Competition Naval Air Weapons Meet at El Centro, California, out-shooting all of the top Naval and Marine pilots in the nation.

Alexander Vraciu's Own Report

Born in East Chicago, Indiana, I won a scholarship to DePauw University, and sensing a war looming on the horizon,

Alexander Vraciu

obtained a private pilot's license under the government's CRI (Civilian Pilot Training) program during the summer vacation between my junior and senior years.

Following graduation in 1941, I entered naval flight training just prior to Pearl Harbor and earned my wings in August, 1942. With planes and aircraft carriers scarce in the earlier phases of the war, I was finally given the opportunity to carrier-qualify on the U.S.S. Wolverine, a converted excursion ship, on Lake Michigan. I qualified on eight straight passes in my F4F Wildcat, demonstrating an early affinity for carrier duty. My first combat assignment was flying F6F Grummans off carriers, learning my deadly trade for five months as wingman to Medal of Honor winner, Lieutenant Commander Edward H. "Butch" O'Hare, Commanding Officer of Fighting Squadron 3 (later changed to 6).

It was while flying section lead in Skipper O'Hare's division that I shot down my first enemy aircraft, a Japanese Zero fighter, at Wake Island in October, 1943. I got a reconnaissance Betty two-engine bomber at Tarawa, and on January 29, 1944, I qualified as an Ace after downing three more Bettys over Kwajalein. The last of these was destroyed after a long, low-level pursuit with only one gun firing part-time at the Betty which was jinking and turning in. I notched three Zeroes and one Rufe in a wild dogfight at the first Truk raid on February 16, 1944, as part of a 72-Hellcat fighter sweep at the Japanese naval fortress. It was a new and enjoyable experience for the F6F pilots, an all-fighter raid with no bombers to protect. That night, Air Group Six, aboard Intrepid, was forced to retire from the combat zone when the carrier was torpedoed by a Japanese Kate.

When my squadron returned to Stateside, I requested continued combat duty. The Navy obliged by assigning me to Fighter Squadron Sixteen aboard Lexington, where I added two more Zeroes at the second Truk raid on 29 April. My 12th kill, another Betty snooper, was shot down north of Saipan on 12 June. Bettys (big, fat-bellied, versatile Japanese bombers) were my prime preoccupation after being told that it was a Betty that had shot down Butch O'Hare on a strange night encounter. On June 14, participating in a strike against enemy shipping in the harbor, I sunk a large enemy merchant ship with a direct hit on its stern.

On 19 June 1 bagged six Judy dive-bombers in eight minutes in what has become known as the Marianas "Turkey Shoot." The following day I shot down a Zero, my last enemy kill, and damaged another while flying escort for bomber and torpedo planes on a record. long-range strike against the Japanese fleet in the First Philippine Sea Battle. Air Group Sixteen was returned to the States, but after several months, I talked my way back out to the combat area when I found that I was being lined up for a War Bond tour. My luck ran out early this time on December 14, 1944, however, when I was shot down by anti-aircraft fire on my second mission while strafing near Clark Field, Luzon, Philippines. After parachuting to safety. I spent the ncxt five weeks with the USAFFE guerrillas and was given the honorary rank of Brevet Major while with them. For the final week of this episode, I found myself in command of 180 men, dodging Japanese to meet General McArthur's advancing Americans. I marched into an American camp sporting a Luger and carrying a Japanese sword. Forced to return home due to regulations, I would not be able to make the first Tokyo raid.

After surviving service on six carriers, two of which were torpedoed, two ditchings and two parachute jumps—to be known as Grumman's Best Customer—my war was over. I was the U.S. Navy's one-time leading Ace for three months in 1944 and ended World War II as the fourth-ranking Naval Ace, having shot down 19 enemy aircraft and destroyed 21 more on the ground. For the last few months of the war I served as a test pilot at the Naval Air Test Center, Patuxent

River, Maryland, helping evaluate tactical performances of U.S. and enemy aircraft.

After post-war staff duty in the Navy Department, Naval Post-Graduate School and shipboard duty, I received the ultimate desire of all fighter pilots—command of my own squadron. As Commanding Officer of Fighter Squadron Fifty-One, I won the High Individual Air-to-Air competition in the 1957 Naval Air Weapons Meet at El Centro, California, outshooting all Naval and Marine pilots for the top honor. I received the following message from CINCPACFLT:
"I AM DELIGHTED TO HEAR THAT YOU ARE TOP GUN IN JETS IN PEACE AS YOU WERE WITH HELLCATS IN WAR X CONGRATULATIONS AND WELL DONE X ADM STUMP."

Vince Mroz • Class of 1941

Vince Mroz has had an extraordinary career in Law Enforcement. He was born in Stanley, Wisconsin. His family moved to East Chicago, Indiana, when he was two years old, where he went to WHS. He was on the football, basketball and track teams. He graduated in 1941 and the same year, he was voted the most outstanding athlete. He then attended Michigan State University under a football scholarship where he was captain of the freshmen

Jules Siegle, coach; Gloria Dosen, East Chicago Room Coordinator; Vince Mroz

football team. In his sophomore year, was the regular left end on the football team.

At the end of his sophomore year, he enlisted in the U.S. Marine Corps and was sent to the University of Michigan, where as a Marine, he lettered in football. In 1943, the University of Michigan was a Big Ten Champion. He has a very distinctive honor of having played for and against the University of Michigan. Vince is a member of the University he of Michigan "M" Club and he served aboard the aircraft carrier, U.S.S. Langley, and the battleship, U.S.S. Iowa. He was discharged after WWII as a first lieutenant. He went back to Michigan State University and completed his degree in criminal justice in 1948.

After graduating from Michigan State, he joined the U.S. Secret Service. He served in Chicago for eleven months and then served in the White House, protecting Presidents Truman and Eisenhower. In 1953, he was transferred to Springfield, Illinois, for 14 months and then back to the White House as a supervisor. After another five years, he was promoted and transferred to Charleston, West Virginia, as Special Agent in Charge handling Secret Service investigation in the entire state.

After three years, he again was promoted and transferred to Kansas City, Missouri, as Special Agent in Charge, handling Secret Service investigations in the 66 western counties in Missouri and the entire state of Kansas. He was transferred back to headquarters in Washington, DC, as an inspector, inspecting the various field offices. After three years, he was again promoted to Deputy Assistant Director of the Uniform Division of the White House Police. Later, when the White House Police responsibilities were expanded to guard the foreign embassies, Vince as Executive Director was in charge of expanding the Uniform Police from 250 officers to 850 officers.

When the Puerto Rican assassins attempted to kill President Truman on November 1, 1950, at the Blair House, Vince was there. In the shoot out, three officers were shot. One was killed and two were wounded. One assassin was killed, and another was wounded and taken into custody. President Truman presented Vince with the Civilian Meritorious Award.

After 26 years in the U.S. Secret Service, Vince retired in 1974. In 1976, Vince went to work with the Montgomery County Public Schools, in Rockville, Maryland, in the Department of Transportation, where he supervised 130 drivers and 25 aids. He retired in 1986.

Vince and his wife, Shirley, moved to Naples, Florida, permanently in 1989 after being "Snow Birds" since 1976.

In 1995, Vince went back to work this time with the Collier County Sheriff's Office. He is supervisor of the Background Investigative Unit, being kept busy, working four days a week.

Vince met his wife Shirley on a blind date while in U.S. Marine Corps Officer's Candidate School. She is from Iowa, and was working for the F.B.I. They married in 1945. They had two children—a daughter, Barbara, and a son, Gregory. Barbara married, had one daughter, and retired from I.B.M. after 25 years. Son Gregory is in the U.S. Secret Service getting ready to retire. He is married and has three children. Vince and Shirley have two great-grandchildren.

Clinton's Pardon Prompts Memories

Archibald McKinlay • Class of 1945 • Chicago, IL

The recent flap about whether President Clinton should pardon Puerto Rican nationalists brings to mind a couple of stories. The first is about Clinton's role model and may be apocryphal. When Vince Mroz, a secret service agent assigned to John F. Kennedy, became alarmed by the nightly parade of beauties in the White House, he warned the president: "All hell is going to break loose if the press ever gets .wind of this." And Kennedy said, "Who would believe it?"

The second story concerns my old friend and sponsor, futurist John Naisbet, whom I once succeeded in a job and who subsequently wrote the best-selling "Megatrends." John, who lives in Telluride, CO, but wanders the world, was making a speech telecast on C-SPAN about staying competitive and surviving in the future. His theme was that the world is becoming a tough marketplace because it is decentralizing for the sake of efficiency—everywhere except the United States. That's ironic since, with our separate states, we practically invented decentralization. Decentralization or not is what the Puerto Rican burr is all about: statehood, status quo or independence. The last group spawns the terrorists.

During the first wave of terrorism almost 40 years ago, the surviving perpetrators were caught and jailed. Years later, they were pardoned by President Jimmy Carter, whom Clinton cites as the precedent for pardoning the present crop. And that gets us back to Vince Mroz, whose story I told in a March 20, 1987, "Calumet Roots." Here it is again:

The Polish midwife stole baby Vincent, sold him, and fled across the border to Russia.

Distraught beyond all rationality, the parents and their relatives virtually ransacked the vicinity in their attempts to recover the infant. It was no use. The baby was gone, and with him a good part of them. So, with trouble of a more universal nature beginning to swirl about them and all of Europe, they packed their belongings and two older boys, John and Stanley, and set off to make a new start in a new world, specifically the quintessential melting pot, Indiana Harbor, where more than 100 nationalities and races lived in surprisingly close harmony.

In this country, Mrs. Mroz delivered three girls: Mary, Veronica and Helen. Then, finally, another boy. The parents named him Vincent, just as the stolen boy had been named. In a few years, Vots (from Wallen for Vincent and its diminutive Volzak), grew into a fine specimen of a man. Six-foot-three and 190 pounds, he starred in three high school sports. Meanwhile, the midwife who had stolen and sold baby Vincent returned from Russia to the Mroz's home town to spend her remaining years. Alas, she found no peace. Mrs. Mroz's persistent brothers recognized her and, after painful confrontations, through her located Vincent, by then an adult. At first, Vincent could not and would not believe that his real parents lived in the Calumet Region of America. But, after extensive personal research, he at last accepted the truth, and the American Mrozes prepared for a reunion. Unfortunately, World War II interfered. A captain in the Polish reserve, Vincent was called to active duty, and when Nazi "panzers" overran Poland in 1939, Vincent vanished.

Vots, for his part, played varsity football for both Michigan State and the University of Michigan, served as a seagoing Marine lieutenant, returned to college to complete his degree, and joined the Secret Service, which eventually led him to the White House. On Nov. 1, 1950, two Puerto Rican nationalists stormed Blair House in an attempt to assassinate President Truman, who was living there while the White House was being renovated. In the hail of bullets that ensued, one White House uniformed officer was killed and two others wounded, and as bullets whistled all about him, Vots serenely fired back at the would-be killers. One took a slug in his chest and survived; the other died instantly. Vince Mroz who may have saved the president's life, was given the highest award his country can bestow for such heroics.

During this same postwar era, the original Vincent suddenly materialized in Poland. After years of hiding in the underground, he surrendered to the Communists who had occupied his homeland. They took no action against Vincent. Neither would they permit him to leave the country. Learning of this, Vots asked President Eisenhower, through his personal secretary Ann Whitman, to intervene, and the president, even in those inflexible days of Cold War, somehow arranged for Vincent to obtain a visa. In 1958, therefore, Vincent arrived onthe S.S. United States, and it was Vots' wife, Shirley, who recognized him first. He was a dead ringer for Vots, except four inches shorter.

John Latko • Class of 1938

John Joseph Latko was born on June 19, 1919, graduated from WHS in 1938, and enlisted in the United States Marine Corps on March 15, 1941, at a time when the Corps was rapidly expanding. John Latko was perhaps the first East Chicago citizen to experience war at first hand, for he was on board the battleship West Virginia (BB-48) at Pearl Harbor on December 7, 1941. By October 1942 he had been promoted to the rank of corporal, and continued to serve in the Marines until August 1945. After the war John returned to Lake County, and eventually joined the Pearl Harbor Survivors' Association.

Walter Mackay • Class of 1937

Walter E. Mackay was born on May 8, 1919, graduated from WHS in 1937, and went to Purdue University for two years, where he studied aeronautical engineering. He entered the U.S. Army on January 29, 1941 and served in the Engineers at Fort Knox, Kentucky, for a year, before transferring to the Air Corps. Walter received his basic training as an Aviation Cadet at Santa Ana, California, and won his commission as a bombardier on December 12, 1942, at Williams Air Field in Arizona. By mid-1943 he was a 2nd lieutenant, and assigned to the 98 Bombardment Group (Heavy), which was equipped with the four-engine Consolidated B-24 "Liberator" heavy bomber.

On August 1, 1943, Walter took part in Operation Tidal Wave, a special low-level attack on the Romanian oil refineries at Ploesti, one of the bloodiest and most dramatic air raids of the war. The 9 Bomb Group put forty-one planes over the target, and all bombed successfully. However, nineteen of those planes were then either shot down or had to "ditch" in the Mediterranean Sea. For his part in Tidal Wave, Walter was awarded the Distinguished Flying Cross. Unfortunately he had only a short time to enjoy that honor, for Walter was killed in action on December 1, 1943. During a bombing raid on Solingen, Germany, his B-24 was shot up by enemy fighter planes and anti-aircraft guns, but managed to reach England where it made a crash landing.

Besides the Distinguished Flying Cross, Walter had received the Air Medal with one oakleaf cluster and the Purple Heart. After the war ended his body was returned to the United States and given a military funeral at the Prusiecki Funeral Home in East Chicago, on July 29, 1948.

Leroy O. Pederson • Class of 1943

LeRoy 0. Pederson was born in 1925, and left WHS a month before graduation in 1943 in order to enlist in the Navy. Discharged after his wartime duty in the Navy's Construction Battalions, or "SeaBees," he enlisted in the U. S. Army in late 1945. LeRoy made a career of the Army, and was in his second six-years hitch when the Korean War broke out. A Private 1st Class, serving with the 13 Engineer Construction Battalion, part of the 7 Infantry Division, he was killed in action on December 1, 1950, one of the first service men from East Chicago to be killed in Korea.

Sigmund L. Toth

Sigmund L. Toth was born in 1925 and attended WHS before enlisting the U. S. Army during World War II. He saw service in Europe, being wounded during the Battle of the Bulge, receiving both the Purple Heart and the Bronze Star. During the Korean War, Sergeant Toth was serving in the 7th Infantry Regiment of the 7 Infantry Division when he was wounded again on September 22, 1950, during combat in Seoul, the capitol of South Korea. After recovering from his wounds, he was promoted to Master Sergeant and returned to duty with his unit. Unfortunately he was then killed in action on April 9, 1951.

Harold Gomez • Class of 1965

Harold Gomez was born in East Chicago on September 30, 1946. One of seven children, he graduated from WHS in 1965, and enlisted in the U. S. Marine Corps that October. After boot camp training at San Diego, Harold was sent to Viet Nam in early 1966. By February 1967 he was a Corporal in the 1st Battalion, 9th Marine Regiment. On February 21, 1967, while serving as a Fire Team Leader with the 2nd Platoon, Company "A," 1st Battalion, in Quang Dien Province, Harold was mortally wounded by an exploding mine. For his outstanding heroism and leadership he was awarded the Silver Star. His other decorations included the Purple Heart, the Presidential Unit Citation, the Combat Action Medal and the Vietnam Service Medal with two bronze stars.

Walter Ronald Dee • Class of 1940

Walter played varsity tennis at WHS and also at Purdue University. Walter received degrees from both Purdue (Engineering) and Northwestern (Finance). He went into the service and became Officer assigned to the Military Intelligence Service of the U.S. Army.

He worked as an engineer at Combustion Engineering

(East Chicago) and as Production Manager of Amgears, Inc. (Chicago). He became a Management Consultant in Chicago and Los Angeles with the largest CPA firm in the world, Peat, Marwick & Mitchell.

He later joined White Stag Co., of Portland, Oregon, makers of ladies and girl's sportswear, skiwear and Speedo swimsuits, as Financial V.P. Walter became the President of White Stag of Canada in Edmonton, Alberta.

He then became President of Liz Carlson Co. (Junior Miss Sportswear) in San Francisco.

In 1959, Walter was chosen as the top member of the Los Angeles Chapter of the National Association of Accountants which had 2,500 members. He had an article published in the 1959 monthly magazine of the National Association of Accountants. The article was voted by the Association as one of the top 10 of some 300 articles published during the year. In 1967, he was President of the Portland Chapter of the National Association of Accountants. In 1968, he was President of the Financial Executives Institute in Portland.

Upon retirement, Walter became very active as a volunteer. Under the AARP/IRS Tax Aid Program, he did hundreds of tax returns free-of-charge for senior citizens and low-income families. He was a Board Member and Financial Consultant for the Retired Senior Volunteer Program of Portland. Walter assisted non-profit agencies in areas of accounting, grants, cash management, office procedures and fiscal controls. For the year ended March 31, 1992, he was named volunteer of the year by the Retired Senior Volunteer Program of Portland.

Locally, he belongs to the Highland Elks and the St. Thomas Moore Knights of Columbus. His hobbies are golf, playing bridge and reading.

Robert C. Haugh • Class of 1939

Born in East Chicago, Indiana, on December 28, 1920, Bob Haugh graduated from WHS in 1939 and entered Indiana University in the fall. He then entered the U.S. Navy in 1942 and served in the Pacific Theater during World War II. After the war, he returned to Indiana University in 1946 and graduated with a B.S. degree in 1948. Upon graduation, he went to work for U.S. Gypsum Company in Indianapolis.

In 1952, he joined New Castle Products as district sales manager and became vice president of sales and executive Vice President over the next 13 years. He moved to Dallas in 1967 as vice president of operations of Overhead Door Corporation and in 1970 became President, CEO and Director. During this tenure, the company grew from a private company of $39 million in sales to a New York Stock Exchange Company with sales of over $400 million. Bob retired in 1990 after 20 years as CEO.

At various times, he has served as a director of the following companies:
- Redman Industries, Dallas
- P.C. Henderson, Ltd., Romford Essex, UK
- Mercantile Bank, Dallas
- Medical City Hospital, Dallas
- Staubach Company, Dallas
- Paul Anderson Youth Home, Dallas
- Robertson Fleet Service, Dallas

He is currently active as director of:
- Baylor Hospital Foundation, Dallas
- Preston Hollow Presbyterian Church Foundation, Dallas
- Metro-Mark Industries, Minnetonka, MN
- White Rock Marathon, Dallas
- Tyler Cup Foundation, Dallas
- Parc Du Loc Homeowners Association, Dallas

Bob was also honored by the Indiana School of Business by being named to Academy of Alumni Fellows in 1983. He was named outstanding alumnus of Delta Upsilon Fraternity in 1982. In 1998, Bob received Indiana University's highest award by being elected for the Distinguished Alumni Service Award. He was inducted into the President's Circle at Indiana in 1999.

Bob has been a strong donor to Indiana University by the following actions.

- The new Indiana University Track and Field Complex was named in his honor in 1997 for his financial contribution.
- The outdoor plaza of the new Indiana Alumni Building was named after Bob and his wife Barbara in 1997.
- As co-chairman of the 1948 class reunion, he led them to a record for money raised by any alumni class.
- He was involved in the building of an improved Weight Room and Training Center that was dedicated in 1998.
- Funded the purchase of a tarp covering for the refurbished Indiana Football Field in 1999.
- A 12th ranking man for his many involvements in supporting the University Athletic Program.

Bob is active in Preston Hollow Presbyterian Church as:

- Director on Executive Committee.
- Member of Finance Committee.
- Member of Building and Grounds Committee.
- Led the effort to retire the church debt.
- Volunteer driver for the Meals on Wheels program.

Bob was married to Barbara Meek, Indiana Class of 1944, who passed away on September 22, 1999. This wonderful marriage produced three daughters and seven grandchildren.

Bob has always been a great believer in physical fitness and its positive effects on being able to handle the stress of modern-day living, and its contributions to a longer and more productive life. He has run 26 marathons, including eight in Boston, four in New York, and four in White Rock. Bob has held two age group records for the 50-mile Ultra Marathon at age 59 and 61. He continues to be a strong advocate of this lifestyle by cycling, snowshoeing, walking and water aerobics. In 1997, he was awarded the Kenneth Cooper prize for Aerobics Leadership. In December of 1999, Bob received the Dallas White Rock Marathon Award for Excellence. This award is given to an individual who has demonstrated a positive effect on health and fitness.

They're Getting Together

By: Frank G. Hanak • Class of 1938 • Griffith, IN

This love story needs to be told during the Valentine season. On May 25th, the night before the 62nd reunion of the class of 1939, sponsored by Bob Haugh, Bob hosted a dinner at Teibel's Restaurant for early arrivals. Some of the classmates that attended this dinner were Jim and Katherine Vlahos, Dick and Betty Walker and Eleanor Pihulic.

I volunteered to take pictures of the event and then leave. Later, I was told it was a great evening of remembering and recalling old friends and classmates they had not seen for many years.

During the reminiscing, Bob Haugh asked, "Whatever happened to Sue Tobias?" Someone said that they had heard she had passed away. Bob remarked that Sue was too beautiful to have died. The next night at the class reunion, the subject of Sue Tobias came up again, but no one seemed to know what had happened to her.

Bob later asked me to verify what had happened to her. After several weeks of research I called Bob with the good news. Sue was very much alive and well in Phoenix, AZ.

Sue's whereabouts were uncovered by a series of phone calls and contacts I made to friends and relatives of Sue. The key was locating a Suzanne Joyce in Florida. Suzanne was the daughter of Jean Tobias Joyce, class of 1937. Jean Tobias Joyce was Sue's older sister who passed away in 1982. Jean and Chuck Joyce had lived in Griffith, IN.

When I reached Suzanne, she was at first reluctant to give me any information about her Aunt Sue, but after reminding her of my son Frederic, and how he played with the Joyce children in Griffith, she knew I was legitimate and gave me all of the information that I needed.

I then called Sue in Phoenix and told her all about the 1939 class reunion and sent her copies of the programs from the reunion and a copy of the ANVIL that featured Bob Haugh. I later called Bob with the good news about Sue. He called her and they had a great conversation of what had happened in their respective lives.

Bob and Sue found out that they had a lot in common. They had both been care-givers for their spouses, which had both passed away after long, debilitating illnesses.

On July 11th, Bob flew to Phoenix, where he spent about six hours with her, including lunch together. In his words, it could not have gone better. She looked great, was in good health, and they were very compatible. They kept in contact by phone, and on September 6th they met at his home in Beaver Creek, CO, for a truly wonderful ten days. Since then, Bob has been back to Phoenix three times with side trips to Sedona and the Grand Canyon. Their getting together has turned out to be an unbelievable turn of events in both of their lives.

It was the class of 1939 reunion that was the catalyst that put them together. They both agree that this has turned out to be a life changing event for both of them as they have fallen head over heels in love with each other! This has turned out to be a real love story.

[Note: A sidebar to the Bob Haugh/Sue Tobias love story: The key to finding Sue Tobias was to find a member of the Jeannie Tobias Joyce family. Both Jean and Chuck Joyce passed away and the large family grew up and moved. I called many people who lived near us and knew of the Joyce family. After twelve to fifteen calls I located Sue's niece Suzzy Joyce in Florida. I related a story to her to solidify my credibility. It was when the Joyce children were pre-schoolers and were playing with my pre-school son, Frederic. He came home and said, "The Joyce kids won't let me play with them." I asked why? He said,
"The Joyce children asked if I am Public or Catholic." I told Frederic that he was a Christian and to go back and play. The Joyce kids accepted this and continued to play together.]

Names to Remember: Milford and Margaret Christenson—From the "Times" Newspaper, Sunday, November 18, 2001

Milford Christenson was born August 12, 1922, and Margaret Christenson was born October 28, 1924. She is a graduate of WHS, class of 1942.

They have been married for 52 years and have two children, six grandchildren and five great-grandchildren. They are Griffith residents. She has a bachelor's degree in public school music from Indiana University in Bloomington and a master's degree in educational media from Purdue University Calumet. She is retired from Griffith Public School Corporation. He has a bachelor's degree in business from Indiana University in Bloomington, and is President of Christenson Chevrolet in Highland. He is a 2001 nominee for "Time" Magazine Quality Dealer Award.

Milford and Margaret Christenson are community-minded and motivated. They actively support their alma maters, serve as board members for the Northwest Indiana

Symphony Orchestra and are active members of First United Methodist Church in Griffith. The couple helped raise money for the church elevator, and Milford has served on the advisory committee. Margaret was choir director for 25 years and continues to share her music expertise as an organist, director of hand bells and as assistant choir director. Milford is a U.S. Army veteran and was a driving force in the acquisition of the army tank for Central Park in the early 1950's. He is a member of American Legion Post 66 and VFW Post 9982 in Griffith. He serves on the Griffith Public School Foundation Board of Directors and served on the Griffith Public School Board and Special Education Cooperative. Milford was a volunteer fireman for Griffith for 25 years and is a member of Griffith Rotary Club and Share Foundation. He also serves on the fundraising advisory board of Hammond Area YMCA and is a contributor at Campagna Academy in Schererville. Margaret and Milford serve on a number of boards at Purdue and IU, and sponsor scholarships at each institution.

Personal Heroes: "People who do something for the community—we think it's important to do for the community, support local community activities and businesses," Margaret said.

Favorite Book/Author: Margaret: "I like to read historical fiction and biographies. Milford sticks mostly to business reading. He subscribes to at least five papers each day."

How to get involved: Community organizations and churches are in need of volunteers.

Advice: "Keep busy and keep doing what you like to do."

People might be surprised to know: Margaret: "We enjoy the arts."

Mary Beth (Johnson) Edelson • Class of 1951 • New York City, NY

When I speak of growing up in the Harbor I want people to know how different this experience was from the majority of white Anglo-protestant girls in the Midwest. I want to talk about what a privilege it was to grow up in one of the most vibrant ethnically and racially mixed cities in mid-20th century America. The grunge and roughness of East Chicago, and the unfinished business of social justice that we witnessed shaped my whole life. Especially living through the labor strikes, and later during the civil rights movement when I learned the tools of activism that I applied to my life-long involvement in the revolution of the feminist movement.

During 7th grade in 1947 I had my first opportunity to test my own mettle when WHS students went on strike against those who opposed racial integration of all the activities in the school—with our winning basketball heroes leading the strike! In the previous summer at my Methodist church camp a Rabbi who had escaped Nazi Germany talked about watching a boxcar burn with his wife inside, and then he deconstructed racism by encouraging us to speak openly about our prejudices so we could see them for what they were. Out of the 2,000 population of WHS, I counted 12 of us who did not go out on strike. Thanks Rabbi, for helping me find the courage.

Johnny (Miss Mildred Johnstone), the best teacher I ever knew, sent me to the principal in 4th grade in the heat of the election between Roosevelt and Dewey. She insisted I remove the Dewey button pinned to my sweater because it was oversized and was causing a stir, but when I complied the cluster of smaller Dewey buttons pinned underneath were revealed, and that was just too in your face for our working-classsteel mill town. Even the thought of Dewey was too much—let alone a display of support. (Disclaimer: of course in

104

4th grade I was under the influence of my parent's political views and not my own.)

Later in high school as part of Johnny's "troop" I wangled passes out of my not-favorite Latin class to design and paint the flats for her productions. This experience proved to be invaluable for a budding artist to learn to paint large scale on canvas, and Latin—well that did not come in handy in future years.

And then there were all the wonderful boyfriends—top among them was Jake Nelson, AKA Arnold Nelson Jr., AKA J.R. I later refereed to him as the best-looking boy from a crime family in WHS, but he was much more than that—a survivor, superb athlete and the first in his family to go to college. And who can forget Johnny Stephinopoulos (8th grade), Joe Himden, (9th grade), Kenny Holmes (10th grade), Gilbert Fernandez, Alex Stamatakis or Sam Korgish; and then everyone had a crush on the illusive Jim Tracey and Henry Gillis.

Since those days I went on to become the artist I wanted to be—the following are published excerpts from press releases and articles on my work:

Mary Beth (Johnson) Edelson—The Artist

Mary Beth Edelson lives and works in New York City. Her work is widely exhibited and critiqued in the U.S. and abroad, and is in the collection of major museums internationally including: Guggenheim Museum, New York, NY; Walker Art Center, Minneapolis, MN; and Museum of Modern Art, New York, NY.

In addition to international recognition, Edelson's work has been discussed in the literature of fields as diverse as psychology, women's studies, photography and theology. Begin-ning as a painter with a master's degree from New York University in the early 1960s—in the 1990s she was awarded an honorary doctorate degree by her alma mater, DePauw

University. While Edelson continued to produce paintings and drawings, her production extended to photography, print-making, installation, sculpture, murals, performances, conceptual works, posters and artists books.

The most extensively reproduced and critically debated of Edelson's work is the poster, *Some Living American Women Artists/Last Supper*. When Edelson created her landmark poster, in 1972, (based on the famous Leonardo di Vinci painting of the last supper) she was questioning the hierarchy and sexism of organized religion by substituting the heads of Jesus and his disciples for the heads of women artists on the poster. Twenty-five years later this poster still arouses controversy; nonetheless, it has been included in numerous major museums exhibitions, and has become the iconic image of feminist art of the 1970s.

Edelson's *Story Gathering Boxes*, begun in 1972, is an ongoing project in which gallery-goers participate by writing their own real stories and leaving them in the story box for others to read. Their participation not only bridges the gap between the viewer and the artwork, but also welcomes them into the art making process.

Currently she has declared that . . . " beginning in January 2003 I will use only supplies that I have on hand or what I am given or find on the street to produce my art works." The first of two projects planned are creating personal altars inspired by the street altars that sprang up in New York City after 9/11. The second project is presenting creative public social space for the purpose of calling attention to the commercial interests that are shrinking public space in our cities.

Since she evokes and visualizes feminine strength, Edelson inevitably provokes criticism from some traditional power brokers, whose influence she eludes by being an accomplished and canny shape-shifter. Indeed Edelson has emerged again and again in new guises—lecturer, explorer of spiritual power, feminist activist (notably Combat Zone against Domestic Violence and in helping to found WAC, the New York-based Women's Action Coalition, which addressed the art world and human rights in its larger international context), and multimedia provocateur.

The recently released book, *The Art of Mary Beth Edelson*, is a 200-page, full color, lavishly illustrated survey of her work and life (including her days in the Harbor). It is available on-line through amazon.com or from the distributor at 800-338-2665 or if you wish an autographed copy, pre-pay $32 (includes shipping) to Seven Cycles, 110 Mercer St, New York, NY 10012.

Carla Rae Johnson • Class of 1965 • Peekskill, NY

Carla Rae Johnson graduated from WHS with the class of 1965. She received a Bachelor of Science degree from Ball State University in Muncie, IN, and a Master of Fine Arts degree from the University of Iowa in 1975. Currently she is a sculptor and an Associate Professor of Art at Marymount College of Fordham University where she is chair of the Fine Arts Unit and the Art Department.

As a sculptor, she has exhibited nationally, in New York City, and in the New York metropolitan area. Her exhibitions have included solo shows in New York City at SOHO 20 Gallery, Ceres Gallery and the Elizabeth Foundation for the Arts. Her work has been featured in exhibitions at The Loveland Museum in Colorado; The Mississippi Museum of Art and the Meridian Museum of Art in Mississippi; The Mead Museum of Art in Amherst, Massachusetts; The Heckscher

Museum of Art in Huntington, New York; The Queens Museum of Art at Paine Webber Art Gallery in New York City; The National Museum of Women in the Arts in Washington, DC; Yale University Art Gallery in New Haven, Connecticut; The Brooklyn Museum of Art; and in numerous college and university art galleries.

In 2002 she was commissioned to design the Cultural Tourism Center for the Arts Exchange Building of the Westchester Arts Council in White Plains, New York. In 1990 she received a fellowship from the Pollock-Krasner Foundation. She has been awarded Artist-in-residencies at the Heckscher Museum of Art in Huntington, New York, and at Studios Midwest in Galesburg, Illinois. Publications highlighting her work have included: the College Art Association's *Abstracts 2003; A Dictionary of the Avant-Gardes, 2nd Edition; Who's Who in American Art; Language as Object: Emily Dickinson and Contemporary Art;* and *Lines of Vision: Drawings by Contemporary Women.* Her work has received notices and reviews from *The New York Times, The New Haven Register, The Village Voice, Women Artist's News, Ceramics Monthly* and numerous local newspapers in the New York metropolitan area. Her work has received several awards. Most recently her sculpture was awarded a "Director's Choice Award" at the 2002 Westchester Biennial at the Castle Gallery in New Rochelle, NY.

In February of this year Carla Rae Johnson will co-chair a panel titled: *Search/Research: Artists in the Archives* at the 2003 National Conference of the College Art Association in New York City. She resides and has her studio in Peekskill, NY, where she is a member a thriving artists' community.

Virtuoso to Play

After her concert in San Diego on December 5, WHS's most accomplished musician ever returned to the Calumet Region for the Holiday Buffet, December 30, 1998, at Woodmar Country Club.

Irene Levy (Alexander) ('37) began playing the piano at the age of 2-1/2. By the time she was 3-1/2, she was the Calumet Region's prime child prodigy, and within a short time would play for Queen Marie of Romania when she visited Chicago. From then on she played more recitals and concerts than Paderewski. She won a state-wide contest that led her to Indiana University to study under Professor Herman Hoffzimmer, and to Northwestern to study under Kurt Wanieck. She then moved on to the American Conservatory of Music to study under Heniot Levy, the world's leading expert on Chopin.

After playing in contest after contest and winning them all, Irene played not only at Chicago's Orchestra Hall but in concerts from coast to coast. Along the way, she studied with the legendary Dr. Rudolph Ganz at the Chicago Musical College and won a recording contest. When Israel opened its national concert hall, she was invited by prime minister David Ben-Gurion to appear, and traveled to the Middle East with Leonard Bernstein. While Bernstein directed the orchestra in the big hall, Irene performed before a number of private audiences. In the process, she became Ben-Gurion's favorite pianist.

Eventually, Dr. Ganz had Irene play for Louis Sudler, the great real estate tycoon, who was board chairman of the Chicago Symphony Orchestra and also sponsored TV's "Artists' Showcase." Thereafter, Irene not only helped Sudler with CSO matters but worked with him on his television show, appearing on it frequently.

When Irene played Town Hall in New York in 1967, another facet of her career threatened to open up. Because the stunningly beautiful Irene was a dead-ringer for Sophia Loren, she attracted crowds wherever she went. This led Otto Peminger, the movie mogul, to court Irene for his movies, while other Hollywood emissaries sought her as a double for Sophia Loren so that the sexy Italian actress could play the part of a great concert artist. Already coping with a full agenda, Irene declined.

During the reign of Mayor Daley, the elder, Irene canceled a European concert tour to accept his invitation to head Chicago's cultural development committee. She is still deeply involved in Chicago's cultural scene.

CHAPTER SIX

6

Sports Stars

Team Champions

1922	Football	State Champions
1927	Basketball	State Runners-up
1930	Baseball	Conference Champions
1931	Basketball	Conference Champions
	Baseball	Conference Champions
	Swimming	Conference Champions
1932	Football	State Champions
1937	Tennis	Conference Champions
	Swimming	State Relay Record Team
1935-1945	Baseball	Conference Champions
1946, 1947	Basketball	Conference Champions
1947	Baseball	Conference Champions
1952	Football	State Champions
1960	Basketball	State Champions
1962	Basketball	Conference Champions
1964	Basketball	Conference Champions
		State Runners-up
1971	Baseball	Conference Champions
1971	Basketball	State Champions
1976	Basketball	State Finalist
1977	Basketball	State Runners-up

Washington High School Athletics Inducted into the East Chicago, Indiana, "Hall of Fame"

Football

Alex Akim
Jim Angelich
Alex Arzumanian
Bill Chamberlain
Nick Cutlich
Joe Gonzalez
Joe Jackura
Luther Keyes

Bill Lovin
Joe Maglish
Hal Method
George Michels
Vincent Mroz
Art Murakowski
Bill Murakowski
Ed Nemeth
Rudy Nicksic

Eugene Opasik
Walter Perko
Alex Sarkisian
Wallace Skierge
Ron Smith
Dimitri Tadich
Robert Turner
Joe Zeller
George Zivich

Basketball

Pete Auksel
Vince Boryla
Junior Bridgeman
Walt Bulatovich
Floyd Campbell
Robert Cantrell

Phil Dawkins
John Dull
Nick Mantis
Richard Mason
Robert Miles
Vic Molodet

Drake Morris
Nick Palla
Anthony Pinkins
Ray Ragelis
George Savanovich
Pete Trgovich

Baseball

Emery Balog
Mike Bajo
Stan Bazan
George Elish
Marshall Fish
Harry Kosinski
Rudy Lomberger
Henry Milton

Joe Pack
Andrew Petterson
Stan Pawenski
Pete Piskol
Chris Platis
Jim Platis
Andy Prieboy
General Rollins

Redell Rollins
George Stepanovich
Fred Stockhaus
Tim Stoddard
George Sufak
Harry Taylor
Matt Tonkovich
Don Yohe

114

Track

Steve Cohen
Henry Gillic
Robert Haugh
Harrington Jackson
Bernard Rivers
Clarence Robinson
Jules Siegle
Wally Smoljian
Monroe Walton

Swimming

Vladimer Haralovich
Dave Mc Cooe
Richard Wurst
Phil Vukovich

Coaches

Travis Buggs
Clifford Freiberger
Thomas Morris
Frank Cash
John McShane
Frank Thomas
Harold Clark
Ernie Miller
Herman Dickes
John Molodet
Nick Sarengach

Boxing

Mike Krizmis
Charles McGregor
Bill Peterson
Mike Primich

Wrestling

Ron Lax
Albert Lummio
George Molodet
Ruben Shehigian
Joe Zeman

Special Category

James Brown
Emilio De La Garza
Frank Casillas
Henry Hardy
Gus Megremis
Philip Ponce
Mary (Platis) Globis
Wilfred Smith
Alex Vraciu
Warren Wiershe

Legends—Best Athletes of All Time 1900 to 1990

Emery Balog
Nick Cudich
Art Murakowski
Alex Srakisian
Joe Zeller
Vince Boryla
Junior Bridgeman
Nick Mantis
Ray Ragelis

Pete Trgovich
Henry Milton
Andrew Patterson
Chris Platis
Jim Platis
Andy Prieboy
Tim Stoddard
Harry Taylor
Don Yohe

Coaches:
John Baratto
John McShane
John Molodet
Frank Thomas

Washington Senators of 1971

Indiana High School State Basketball Champions, undefeated and ranked one of the "best teams ever," if not the best, averaged close to 100 points per game. Coached by John Molodet, three members of this team entered the East Chicago, Indiana, Hall of Fame, and Pete Trgovich, Tim Stoddard and Junior Bridgeman have joined Coach Molodet in the "Legends" category as the very best.

Tim Stoddard • Class of 1971

Played three years varsity for the Senators in football, basketball and baseball. Was on the 1971 WHS undefeated basketball state champions, one of the state's greatest if not the best of all time. All Conference, All State, Kentucky-Indiana All Star team; one of Northern Indiana's leading pitchers; "Times" Athlete of the year.

John Molodet • Class of 1945 • Coach

Coached the freshman and "B" team for 13 years under Coach John Baratto before taking over the reins. His freshman record was an astounding 165 wins and 9 losses in ten years, including 5 undefeated seasons and a 76-game winning streak, a 94% winning percentage. Coach of Year in 1971. Assistant under Baratto on 1960 State Champs and 1962 State Runner-Up teams.

Junior Bridgeman • Class of 1971

Considered along with Vince Boryla to be the greatest basketball player to come out of East Chicago in the city's history. He was on the great 1971 Washington State Championship Basketball Team, going unbeaten 29-0, and averaging, as a team, 91 points per game. He played thirteen years in the NBA.

Pete Trgovich • Class of 1971
Played on the great Senator State Championship Team of 1971. Leading scorer, All Conference, All State, Indiana All Star Team, played on three great UCLA Wooden-coached national teams, on two National Championship Teams. Played on the Walton-led club that won 88 straight games. Signed with San Diego of the ABA pro league.

Nick Mantis • Class of 1955
Played in the mid 1950's under Coach John Baratto. Nick Mantis averaged 27.0 points per game his senior year, a record that still stands. He made the "Chicago Daily News," "Chicago American" and "Chicago Tribune" All Star Teams for two consecutive years, All Northern Indiana twice, and "Parade" Magazine "All American." Played three years at Northwestern University.

Vic Molodet • Class of 1952
Considered the best guard in northern Indiana in 1949 and 1950. All Conference two years, All State mentioned. Starred for three years at North Carolina State. He was All Conference, Honorable Mention All American, and the Wolfpack's Most Valuable Player. He was inducted into North Carolina Hall of Fame.

Vince Boryla • Class of 1944
Played three years for the Senators, All Conference senior year, after graduation went to Notre Dame and rose to stardom overnight. At one time, he held the single season Irish scoring record. Two-time AAU All American with the Denver Nuggets, also All American at Denver University. One of the few athletes ever to be All American at two different universities.

Art Murakowski • Class of 1943
Played three varsity years at WHS; state champions in 1942, All Conference and All State, after Navy service went to Northwestern University. Also played for the famous Great Lakes Naval Training Station during his time in the armed forces. Played three years varsity as a fullback and linebacker for the Wildcats, won the Big Nine Silver Football as Most Valuable player. Played one year with Detroit Lions.

Jim Platis • Class of 1945
In a sense, Jim had two athletic careers (see page 122); beginning in 1983, Jim has had a phenomenal track and field career. He has won 18 gold medals in the National Senior Olympics, was selected Best Performer at the World Senior Olympics in Spain (1992) and Australia (2000), has 283 Masters All American certificates, 55 National #1 rankings, 47 World #1 rankings and 188 World Standards.

119

Indiana State Champions 1942-1943

Top row: Coach Zitko, Mr. Kendall, Coach Pack. Second row: Konefal, Bulla, Hinton. Third row: Fliter, Delor, Jackura, Macera, Bridgeman, Hardy. Fourth row: Adamchik, Chamberlain, Nemeth, Jones, Lucas, Trimble, Tumlin, Keyes. Bottom row: Kish, Perko, Arzumanian, Murakowski, Michels, Stepanovich, Johnson, Gearring.

Front row: Padilla, Holland, Rabatin, Bulfa, Wilmot, Michael, Korotky, Perko. Second row: R. Perry, D. Perry, Fox, Griffin, Bridgeman, Keyes, Costa, Smoth, Brokemond, Seto, G. Stepanovich. Third row: Toth, D. Stepanovich, Morris, Williams, Glasper, Wilson, Jackson, Morgan, Costanza . Top row: Coach Zitko, Mr. Patrick, Ponce, Comer, Lozano, Coach Siegle.

120

Ray Ragelis • Class of 1947

Led the Senators to two sectionals, two regionals and one semi-state championship in high school in 1946 and 1947. All Conference two years, All State, Indiana All Star Team, leading scorer of the state in 1947. Starred at Northwestern University for 3 years, All Big Ten twice, All American mention, Most Valuable Player of Northwestern. Played one year in NBA.

Andy Prieboy • Class of 1948

Probably the best pitcher in East Chicago, Indiana, history for high school performance. Threw six no-hitters, seven one-hitters, All Conference two years, State Legion Champs; signed a big bonus with the Detroit Tigers, worked himself up to Triple A ball with Toledo, played three years with them, hurt arm, should have made it. Charter member E.C. Hall of Fame.

Emery "Buddy" Balog • Class of 1946

A three-sport star in football, basketball and baseball, three years Baseball Conference Champions, All Conference two years, played on the Post 266 State Champions in American Legion, All District, All State, was "Most Valuable Player," played two years in a row at Lake Forest College in all three sports, played at Northwestern and Indiana Universities, was on eight Indiana State Championship teams in amateur baseball.

121

John Baratto • Coach

Coached at WHS for 25 years, won 484 games while losing 170 for a 79% winning record which included 13 sectionals, 9 regionals, 5 semi-states, 1 state runner-up, and 1 state championship. Was Indiana Coach of the Year, was inducted into the state high school Hall of Fame as well as a charter member of the E.C. Hall of Fame.

Jim Platis • Class of 1945

Three-time baseball conference champions, batting champ 1944, Legion State Champs, All State, All Midwest, Best Outfielder Award, 40 times Amateur State Champions, 19 times All State, two times All American, two World Champion Runners-Up, twelve times League batting champion, 18 times Masters Track and Field All American, Nine World Records, 45 times ranked # 1 in the country.

Chris Platis • Class of 1945

Three-time baseball conference champions, Legion State and Midwest Champions, All State and All Midwest, Big Ten Baseball Champions at Indiana University, 40 times Amateur State Champs, three times All American, 18 times All State, two times World Champion Runners-Up, 13 times League batting champion, three times Masters Track and Field All American, three World Records.

122

Joe Zeller • Class of ??

East Chicago Roosevelt and WHS. One of a few athletes who played for both schools. Played in 1926, 1927 and 1928, All Conference and All State, went to Indiana University where he played football and basketball. Was captain of the Hoosier basketball squad in 1931, he also lettered 14 times in baseball and track at Indiana. Was most Valuable Player at Indiana his senior year in football. Played eight years with the Chicago Bears.

Henry Milton • Class of 1930

Played with Andrew Patterson in the early 1930's, on three conference baseball championships. A consistent .350 hitter, great speed and arm. Played eight years with the Kansas City Monarchs of the Negro American League. Would rank among the top five outfielders of all time that came from the northern Indiana area.

Frank Thomas • Coach

Was a star high school football quarterback for the Senators and led them to the city's first state football championship in 1915; went to Notre Dame and played three years under the legendary Coach Knute Rockne. Played Alongside George Gipp and later played with the famous Four Horsemen. Frank is left in picture.

Andrew Patterson • Class of 1931

Along with Henry Milton, also played three years under Coach John McShane in the early 1930s, was on three conference baseball championships. After high school went to college where he was a great star athlete in football, basketball and baseball. Played pro ball for the famous Kansas City Monarchs for many years. Capable of playing Major league baseball if allowed to.

Mike Primich • Class of ??

Was an all-around athelete back in 1928, came in third place in diving at the state meet, and won a second place medal in the state wrestling championship; but his main forte was boxing. This 118-pound package of dynamite almost won a world championship. He won a prestigious Golden Glove title, won of 52 amateur fights and 78 professional fights.

John McShane • Class of ?? • Coach

He too was a highly successful three-sport athlete and was on the Senators 1915 state football champions under legendary Coach Frank Thomas: came back after graduating college and coached football, basketball and baseball at WHS. Charter member, East Chicago Hall of Fame.

Harry Taylor • Class of 1931
Played three years at WHS under Coach John McShane in the late 1920s on three conference baseball championships; signed with the Washington Senators right after high school and played five pro seasons with the club. A great hitter and classy fielder. Charter member, E. C. Hall of Fame.

Alex Sarkisian • Class of 1941
All Sate in football and wrestling at WHS. After World War I played three years at Northwestern University in Evanston. He was All Big Ten, All American, captain, Rose Bowl Champions. Indiana College Football Hall of Fame (South Bend); charter member, E. C. Hall of Fame.

Monroe Walton • Class of 1929
One of the best atheletes to ever graduate from the Senator bastion, and one of the classiest men ever. A great track star in high school and college, charter member of the East Chicago, Indiana Hall of Fame.

Nick Cutlich • Class of 1936

Played three years for the Senators in the mid 1930s, was All Conference and All State, was on the Senator 1932 State Football Champs, also Indiana State Wrestling Champ. Went to Northwestern University where he starred for three years on the Wildcat team, All Big Ten and All American honors. Charter member, E. C. Hall of Fame.

Don Yohe • Class of 1937

Played and starred for three years in the mid-1930s, on three conference baseball and football championships; also starred in basketball. Was signed by the Chicago White Sox and played shortstop the entire exhibition season. He spent several years in the high minors, returned home and starred for the outstanding Inland Steel clubs. He is a member of the E.C. Hall of Fame

Kenny Lofton • Class of 1985

An absolutely outstanding athlete. He made significant contributions to Harbor Little League baseball. A street has been named for him. A remarkable performer at Washington, he played in the final four NCAA tourney for Arizona. A stellar major leaguer, Kenny has played for Cleveland, the White Sox and is now (2003) with Pittsburgh. Last year he was in the World Series with the San Francisco Giants. (Photo Courtesy of Chicago White Sox.)

1932 State Football Champs

In the last of four practice games, the Senators lost to the Bronson Hall gridders in a very hard fought encounter.

The next three games on the maroon and white grid schedule were against the Froebel Blue Devils, the Horsemen of Horace Mann and the Whiting Oilers. For the first time in twelve years the Senators defeated the Blue Devils of Froebel and continued on their campaign of victory by defeating the Horsemen and the Oilers. In these three games, Stan and Rollins each made two touchdowns, Kaslevich and Klokoski made one apiece, and Daronatsy drop-kicked four times over the cross bar for extra points.

The Hammond Wildcats were the next to crumble before the attack of the Senator grid machine. The Cats made two touchdowns in the first five minutes of play, but after that the whole game belonged to the Washingtonians. Daronatsy made the first touchdown for the Senators and Klokoski and Stan followed his example and plunged over the goal line.

The maroon and white eleven was defeated by the Golden Tornado of Emerson. Klokoski made the only good touchdown for the Senators when he hit the center of the line and plunged through. To make up for this defeat, the Senators humbled the Rough Riders of Roosevelt to win the city championship. In this game Stan made two markers and Rollins, racing the length of the field, made a third. Daronatsy drop-kicked twice over the bar for extra points.

The last game for the Washington gridmen of 1932 was against the Blue Avalanche of Elkhart for the Northern Indiana High School football championship. Elkhart drew first blood in the opening quarter and Washington got a safety when White fell upon the ball behind the goal line. The Senators rallied in the second half and Stan made a touchdown after the Senator backs had smashed the Elkhart line to pieces. In the last quarter Stan made another marker, after Daronatsy and Klokoski had brought the ball down the held.

Seven games of their hard, muscle-bruising, eleven-game schedule were won by the Senators' now famous last-half, last-quarter and even last-minute rallies. Seven games! "They didn't even know when they were beaten."

The Senators win the Northern Indiana High School championship.

Indiana Hall of Famers

IN 2002, three WHS alums were inducted into their respective Indiana Hall of Fame. Jake Arzumanian, ('49) entered the Baseball Hall of Fame and Bob Cantrell and "Pop" Miles entered the Basketball Hall of Fame.

Chapter Seven

7

Memories from the 1920s

Believe it or not, there still are a few alums around who attended WHS in the Roaring Twenties. Some who are current members of the WHS Alumni Assn. include: Stacia Skretny Plewa ('23), Jean Templeton ('26), John Bobilik ('29) and Sarah Goodman Goldberg ('29). Even had we not had a communication from an alum of that decade, we would still add a comment ar two about that era, because it was in that decade WHS officially began to serve the community. We begin each decade with a quick summary of the decade's highlights. It's interesting to compare average wages of 1925 and the cost of some everyday items with those of the 1930's. One must not forget what happened in 1929; and 1935, our next comparison year, was probably the very worst year of the Depression. Life expectancy was 54.1 years.

Calvin Coolidge was our President, and Charles Dawes of Indiana was the vice-president. The movies were still silent in 1925, and some of the hits were: "The Gold Rush," "The Big Parade," "The Ghost of Moulin Rouge" and "Go West." Popular songs of that era included: "Sweet Georgia Brown," "Moonlight and Roses," "If You Knew Suzie Like I Knew Suzie," "Five Foot Two, Eyes of Blue" and "Alabamy Bound."

The Indianapolis 500 was won by Peter De Paolo with a speed of 101.3 mph. Pittsburgh won the World Series, and Notre Dame beat Stanford in the Rose Bowl 27-10. Current media personalities born in 1925 include Paul Newman, Peter

Graves, Tony Curtis, Angela Lansbury, Johnny Carson and
Wm. F. Buckley.

Other interesting data from that year:

Average income	**$2,239.00**
New car	**$290.00**
New house	**$7,809.00**
Loaf of bread	**$0.09**
Gallon of gas	**$0.12**
Gallon of milk	**$0.56**
Gold per oz.	**$20.67**
Silver per oz.	**$1.09**
Dow Jones avg.	**134.00**

Superintendent's Letter to Anne Kodicek (Feldman) • Class of 1927 • Deerfield Beach, FL

I received this letter when I was a senior at WHS seventy-five
years ago. It's interesting, you may keep it for the archives.
Thank you for the ANVIL. [The original will be stored in the
East Chicago Room at the EC library, The Editors.]

To the Seniors of 1927

Graduation day looms up in the distance. In your life's journey
the vision of this event is as that of "The Delectable
Mountains" to "Christian" in "Pilgrim's Progress," or like the
vision, (often a mirage), of the oasis to the traveler over desert
wastes. I do not mean to imply that your high school life is
comparable to the experiences of the characters above referred
to. Really you have been in green fields, beside "rivers of
water," and under the watch care of "Good Shephards." And
yet, your achievements are and have been commensurate to
your own efforts. And this must ever be. We hope you have

learned this lesson most thoroughly. "We build the ladder by which we rise." There is no royal road to either learning or success. The important consideration for each of you for the future is to find a way which shall be to you an "open road," not a "blind alley," and then strive forward. To some, this may mean a place, immediately, in the world's work; to others it means some years in college.

I wish to commend your serious thought the following:

THE TEN MARKS OF AN EDUCATED MAN

Albert E. Wiggam, famous lecturer and writer, gives the following as the ten marks of an educated man:

1. He keeps his mind open on every question until all the evidence is in.
2. He always listens to the man who knows.
3. He never laughs at new ideas.
4. He cross-examines his daydreams.
5. He knows his strong point and plays it.
6. He knows the value of good habits and how to form them.
7. He knows when not to think, and when to call in the expert to think for him.
8. You can't sell him magic.
9. He lives the forward-looking, outward-looking life.
10. He cultivates a love of the beautiful.

Sincerely,

J.W. Asbury,

Supt. of Schools.

CHAPTER EIGHT
8
Memories From The 1930s

In 1935, the mid-point of the decade, Franklin Roosevelt was President; John Garner was the Vice-President. There was no minimum wage, and the life expectancy was 59.7 years. Social Security was enacted in 1935. The DC-3 made its maiden flight.

The best picture of the year was "Mutiny on the Bounty." Receiving Oscars for best actor were Victor McLagen in the "Informer" and Betty Davis in "Dangerous" for best actress. Other pictures of that decade were: "Frankenstein," "The Bride of Frankenstein," "42nd Street," "Bringing Up Baby," "Gone with the Wind," "Modern Times," "Duck Soup," "Mr. Smith Goes to Washington," "The Public Enemy," "The Rules of the Game," "Top Hat," "Trouble in Paradise" and "The Wizard of Oz."

Some of the popular songs of the decade were: "Beer Barrel Polka," "Body and Soul," "Cheek to Cheek," "Cocktails for Two," "Easter Parade," "Friendship," "Got a Date with an Angel," "Heart and Soul," "I Didn't Know What Time it Was," "My Ideal," "My Romance," "South of the Border," "Two Sleepy People," and "You Oughta be in Pictures."

Other interesting data from that year:

Average income	**$1,632.00**
New car	**$625.00**
New house	**$3,400.00**
Loaf of bread	**$0.08**
Gallon of gas	**$0.10**
Gallon of milk	**$0.47**
Gold per oz.	**$20.67**
Silver per oz.	**$0.38**
Dow-Jones avg.	**120.00**

My First Day of School at Washington Elementary

Josephine (Bacevich) Gustaitis Booth • Class of 1934 • Schererville, IN

I had just passed my 6th birthday. I had escaped Kindergarten, and in those days, there was no TV, no Sesame Street, no Play School, nothing to prepare me for that day. In all the six years I had never been out of the neighborhood and I was headed for a place unknown.

The moment arrived, my older sister took me by the hand, and away we went—four long blocks away. We arrived and she immediately dropped me off in a line of strange children and abandoned me. Then came the teacher; horrors, she was a witch! Miss Shay had graying hair, disarrayed, wearing small silver glasses and a voice that boomed. I literally froze with fright. Then she had us march into the building, a monster-size, ugly, red-brick structure. We marched through the door and behold, there was this immense set of stairs; I had never seen anything like it. I was so frightened, I could hardly walk up and halfway up I felt a trickle between my legs. I wanted to die, then, like a storm, Miss Shay spotted me, grabbed me by the hand and raced me up and deposited me into a chair, plunked me down, then told me where the toilets were. When I returned home, 1 never told anyone about my horrendous experience.

As the weeks went by at school, all was well. At the end of the year, I was "teacher's pet," and I made more gold stars than anyone in the class.

As the years went by, I loved school. Being a very determined person, I did well. All my grades were straight A's. On graduation day, I had attained my goal. I became Valedictorian of my class and was awarded the Gold Medal, which I still wear occasionally on my charm bracelet. P.S. it is 10K gold!

From an Anonymous Alum

We used big scissors to cut figures out of colored paper and pasted them on whole sheets of another color. We used paste made by ourselves of flour and water. Sometimes it was lumpy.

We learned to use tools in wood shop and I remember proudly presenting my mother with a foot stool that wobbled only a little. It was stained deep brown.

In print shop, we learned to set type and use the old press. The ink disc had to be covered with just the right amount of ink and rolled on carefully.

I remember throwing switches in electric shop and can still connect wires in series to doorbells and light bulbs.

I've loved tools ever since. The wife says I'm tool-crazy, but she'll admit I'll tackle anything; not always success-fully. The house bears evidence everywhere of my handiwork. Some of it can't be seen, but I know it's there. It's all owed to Washington.

Music appreciation and creative writing were tough, but that's another story.

[Editor's note: This will be the last anonymous letter we will publish!! No name, no printed article!]

Recollections from 1937

The following Alumni Association members were part of the Class of 1937: Albert Wiersbe, Munster, IN; William Sabo, Hebron, IN; Freida (Hankins) Johnson, Hammond, IN; Josephine (Jeorse) Vintila, Phoenix, AZ; Donald Dobbie, Prescot Valley, AZ; John Milasich, New Port Ritchey, FL; Christopher & Stoma Monroe, Gary, IN; Henry Koehler, Hammond, IN; Charles Sandor, Hammond, IN; Irene (Pakropinski) Sargovetz, Munster, IN; Charlotte (Roller) Anderson, Dyer, IN; Ann Dickson, Herkimer, NY; Irene (Levy) Alexander, Chicago, IL; Mary (Wagner) Simpson, San Clemente, CA; Irene Bossinger, Merrillville IN; Frank DeRosa Highland, IN; Quentin Rudolph, San Antonio, TX; Wenton Hedinger, Ft. Myers, FL; Ann (Evanson) Goodman, Munster, IN; and Dr. Mary (O'Meara) Tilka, Schereville, IN.

They shared a time filled with happy memories, listening and dancing to such hit songs as: "Harbor Lights," "I've Got My Love to Keep Me Warm," "Johnny One Note," The Lady Is a Tramp," "My Funny Valentine," "The Donkey Serenade," "Whistle While You Work," "In the Still of the Night," "Where or When" and "Thanks for the Memory."

The worst of the Depression Years appeared to be over. A favorite pastime was attending the movie theaters. Some box office stars of the day were: Shirley Temple, Clark Gable, Robert Taylor, Bing Crosby, William Powell, Jane Withers, Sonja Henie, Gary Cooper, Myrna Loy, Fred Astair and Ginger Rogers.

Amelia Earhart was lost at sea. Her around-the-world flight ended somewhere over the Pacific.

Back home fifteen General Motors plants were closed down by strikes. Our U.S. Steel Plant avoided a strike by agreeing to guarantee a minimum wage of $5.00 a day.

At WHS, the SENIOR ANVIL was being prepared by the following classmates: Alex Vraciu, editor-in-chief; Agnes Otvos, art editor; Cosino Demeduke, drawings; Edward Spaulding, Anne Gheaja, John Monea, literary editors; Irene Bajusz, Helen Anderkovics, typists; Marie Gennan, secretary/treasurer; James Malony, Tom Castino, advertising managers; Mary Moldovan, Clara Sirigas, circulation managers; Bill Sabo, Marsha Sostik, Sulo Ranta, John Vana, photography; and Richard Dejerf, business manager.

In national sports 23-year-old Joe Louis defeated James J. Braddock. Joe DiMaggio and the New York Yankees won the World Series. Basketball teams in the Midwest formed the NBA.

Back home the alums listened to radio shows such as "The Chase and Sanborn Hour" with Charlie McCarthy and his sidekick, Edgar Bergan. Radio shows that premiered that year were: "Mr. Keen," "Tracer of Lost Persons," "The Guiding Light," "Stella Dallas," "Grand Central Station," "Big Town" and "Dr. Christian."

This was the year of the Hindenberg disaster. At the Paramount Theatre in New York City, 3,000 teenagers lined up on the street for a chance to see and hear Benny Goodman and His Band.

Back at WHS, the following art students contributed health posters to the clinic: Eleanor Dudzik, Herbert Southern, Mildred Valach, Harriet Bielski, Pearl Davidson, Bernice Rapacz, Lynn Cowan, Frank Vargo and Bertha Gavora.

Coach Schweingruber complimented John Kocur on his fine record of attendance at practice. He hadn't missed a practice in four days!

It was a pity that Azad Sarkisian had such big fingers. His senior ring was so big that Gwen Sargent had to wrap about a yard of string around a part of it to keep it from falling off her finger.

Tony Vega, Washington's foremost weightlifter, held a National A.A.U. title. He formed an arch by supporting himself upon the back of his neck and his feet. This is hard enough for anyone to do, but to top it off; Tony lifted a weight of 315 lbs. straight up while in this position.

Mamie Kiralova represented the WEEKLY ANVIL as a guest reporter at the Red Cross banquet. Helen Stadnick was elected president of the Dress Design Club. Irma Jean Romer was vice president, Genevieve Movdrazak was secretary and Louis Newmark was program chairman. The sponsor for that club was Miss Thrasher, sewing instructor at WHS.

Vera Hedinger, a popular senior, had an audition with the new broadcasting studio in Hammond (WHIP) and was given a program. Vera appeared at many affairs and was given much applause.

Ramon Oliverio, former student of Washington Irving in Clarksburgh, WV, became a senior at WHS. Mr. Robinson was principal. Do you remember some of these teachers? Mr. Altenderfer, Mr. Fauber, Mr. Pratt, Mr. McShane, Mr. Dickes, Mr. Schweingruber, Mr. Clark, Miss Wall, Miss Gaber, Miss Oilar, Miss DePew, Miss Swindell, Mr. Paul, Miss Roomer, Mr. Sievert, Mr. McCoy, Mr. Walley, Miss Overpeck, Mr. Kellem, Miss Mendenhall, Mr. Brunswick, Miss Kozacik, Miss Mills, Mr. Reeves, Miss Sowerby, Mr. Geddes, Mr. Palmer, Miss Shearer, Mr. Tritt and Mr. White.

Michael Spaulding was class president, Marie Banjavic was secretary and Donald Yohe was vice president. Arliss Fuhrmark and John Vana were voted Most Promising while Peter Kolas and Anne Saho were chosen Mr. & Miss Washington.

Some of the local businesses of the day were: Dan Dee Cafe, 3406 Michigan Ave.; Wallace Coal Co., 3509 Guthrie; Albert's Jewelers, Broadway & Main; Gordon Motor Sales, 1508 Broadway; Ford Sales & Service, 1901 Broadway; Twin

City Cleaners, 3515 Parrish; Washington Lumber & Coal, 1109 E. Columbus Dr.; Goodman Drug Co., 3502 Main St.; Harbor Furniture, 3729 Main; Indiana Harbor Ice & Coal, 3509 Guthrie; Straight Radio & Refrigeration, 3460 Michigan; P. Marovich, 3506 Main; Gould's Dept. Store, 3735 Main; Harbor Motors, 3440 Michigan; Central Drug Store, 3410 Michigan; Leo Peters, 3822 Main; Hurwich Furniture, 3424 Michigan; Joe Title & Sons, 3706 Main; Harry Tarlers Shoe Store, 3425 Michigan; Joe Broh, Main; and Nagdeman Bros., 3409 Michigan.

Judy and I Missed Our Own Wedding Reception

Frank Hanak • Class of 1938 • Griffith, IN

In late 1942, 1 was inducted in the Army and was shipped to Ft. Barancas located inside the huge Pensacola Naval Base in Pensacola, Florida.

In January, 1943, I sent a Western Union telegram to my fiancée Judy Rzepczynski proposing marriage and instructing her to bring food ration books and gas ration coupons with the alarm clock. Judy was 20 and I was 22. We still have the telegram. She arrived on January 26, 1943 on the old Monon & L & N Railroad. She came down to tell me to wait until after the war. I arranged with our Colonel, the Battalion Commander, for the wedding in the post chapel. He agreed and ordered the entire battalion (670 soldiers and officers with their ladies) to attend. Moral was low and he being a southern gentleman arranged for a Catholic and Lutheran Chaplain, and also the Battalion Band. I arranged for Dan Medrea, class of 1938, and Jim O'Hara of Roosevelt basketball team to be my best men.

The wedding was set for 6:00 pm. The train was late and the Escambia County Court House closed at 5:00 pm. The old county clerk agreed to wait in the coffee shop across from the court house until Judy arrived.

Lt. Alfred let me use his 1940 Chevy. The train was a half-hour late. I explained to Judy that the wedding was arranged and she could not let the U.S. Army down. After much discussion, the very tired Judy agreed. The clerk then told us that by Florida law, without her parents consent she needed two adults who knew her for five years to verify her character and parental consent. I went outside the Court House and called two Brooklyn G.I.s waiting for a bus to verify the court's request. All the clerk needed was two signatures on the papers. We received our license and went to the Post with the two soldiers in tow. I had a room rented in town and we stopped off for Judy to shower and change into her wedding suit.

When we arrived at the Chapel, the entire battalion and the band were waiting. We received a great ovation and the small chapel was overflowing with soldiers.

After the ceremony, we exited the Chapel under crossed rifles. The Master Sergeant came in and said the Colonel had a reception for us at his home on the bijou. Judy and I could not believe that after only a few months of knowing me, the Colonel would do this. We got into the Chevy and went to the San Carlos Hotel in Pensacola for our wedding dinner. Being a Navy town, the dining room was full of Naval officers. Judy looked great with her large corsage and beautiful smile. The head waiter knew we were just married and he told the Naval officers. They honored us by paying for the entire dinner with beverages. We retired to our room and three days later returned to the camp. My three-day pass was up.

On my arrival, I was ordered to see a furious Commanding Officer. He said, "Frank, you little SOB, you failed to attend your own wedding reception. I should throw you in the brig." He was writing as he was talking and threw the paper at me and said, "Get the hell out of here you little bastard!"

I looked at the paper. It was another three-day pass. I gave him a snappy salute and went on our honeymoon.

Career Predictions for the 1939 WHS Grads

We got this communication from Chris Christoff of the WEEKLY ANVIL's analysis of the 1939 Senators. One wonders how many of the predictions even came close. The following is his column:

The seniors are leaving. Therefore, this entire column will be dedicated and given over to them. They are now going out into the wide, wide world. Here are just a few predictions as to what will become of them: Stella Jurevich—A second Maude Adams; Chuck Boyd—Mr. Average Man; Steve Yavore—Machine Gun Tommy; Tony Ancich—a law-enforcing cop; Doris Freedle—a famous female lawyer; Victoria Vangeloff—a comfortable housewife; Meyer Evanson—a newsreel photographer; Robert Haugh—a clothes' designer; Tom Blosky—an erratic inventor; Jack Blosky—Cubs new shortstop; Irene Tansas—a bright plaid skirt; Mary Sedor—a chewy grin with gum; Dick Walkowiak—a little toy gun and cocked hat; Joe Kolady—a hatful of tricks and a bag of wind; Joe Barbush—a soothing disposition; Ethel Szoke—an unknown quantity; George Banjavic—an idiotic giggle and a heart of gold; Esther Berkovitz—Madame La Berk; Steve Muntean—Captain in the reserve army; Wanda Aranoski—a pert stenographer; Lorraine Lewis—a charming society patron; John Turean—just a journalist; Dan Strapon—head of a cooking school; Phyllis Burke—dean of a girl's school; Elsie Fenske—a famous milliner; John Hitra—a super salesman; Ray Edinger—an executive; Rose Georgieff—secretary to the president; Lucille Turich—eminent doctor of surgery; Curtis Patterson—school teacher; Teresa Dominick—head librarian of the Congressional Library; Angeline Slazyk—an adventur-

Graduation June 8, 1939

(L to R) Mary Ergrzan, Mary Chicki, Nick Sholomitz

(L to R) Louise Ammon, Luse Baker, Mike Lipay

142

ess; Josephine Guzis—physical education instructor; George Germek—Councilman of the 4th ward; Bill Simolin—foreign correspondent; Danny Williams—Daniel Williams, M.D.; Marjorie Manker—competitor of Lily Pons; Earl Lind—a second Grover Whalen; Emma Skrtic—some executive's spouse; S. Rosenbloom—an absent-minded professor; Mamie Kirilova—the gay divorcee.

Well, do you agree with me? No? You should, I think those are fairly close. But time alone will tell, of course.

The Magic of Washington High School

Lillian (Frye) Van Kempema • Class of 1938 • Crown Point, IN

I knew I wanted to teach, and I knew I wanted to return to Washington High School for that. And so it was . . . After three years Wally and I were married, but there was a school board policy of not hiring married women teachers. I dutifully resigned, but there was a war on and teachers were scarce, so I was rehired. My husband's plea to join him in the State of Washington took precedence and I resigned at the end of the first semester in 1946.

It was not until 1955 that I returned to teaching as a substitute in grades 1-8. 1 didn't know "how to be a sub" because I did everything a full-time teacher would do and it wasn't long before I had a full-time contract was in my hands, working with 7th and 8th grade students.

I fell in love with this new responsibility and soon was offered a counseling position in which I remained for almost 20 years. All my years of teaching were most gratifying and enriched my life because children came to school to learn, teachers wanted to teach, and parents were most supportive.

Working on class reunions has been one way of keeping alive friendships of long ago. A stroke (TIA), and then an

MVA (caused by a man who totaled my car and another) has slowed me down a bit, but I'm a fighter and expect to be on the golf course again before winter sets in.

For All Those Born Before 1945*

Nick Pope • Class of 1936 • Norfolk, VA

We are survivors! Consider the changes we have witnessed: We were born before television, before penicillin, before polio shots, frozen foods, Xerox, plastic, contact lenses, frisbees and the pill. We were before radar, credit cards, split atoms, laser beams and ballpoint pens. Before pantyhose, clothes dryers, electric blankets, air conditioners, drip-dry clothes and before man walked on the moon.

We got married first and then lived together. How quaint can you be? In our time, closets were for clothes, not for "coming out of." Bunnies were small rabbits, and rabbits were not Volkswagens. Designer jeans were scheming girls named Jean, and having a meaningful relationship meant getting along with our cousins.

We thought fast food was what you ate during Lent, and Outer Space was the back of the Indiana Theater. We were before house-husbands, gay rights, computer dating, dual careers, and commuter marriages. We were before day-care

Harbor Memories: School starts next week!

IT'S ALMOST TIME FOR SCHOOL... THIS YEAR JIM WILL GET JOE'S FROM LAST YEAR, JACK WILL GET JIM'S. WE'LL SEE WHAT YOUR COUSINS HAVE FOR SUSIE.

centers, group therapy and nursing homes. We never heard of FM radio, tape decks, electronic typewriters, artificial hearts, word processors, yogurt and guys wearing earrings. For us, time-sharing meant togetherness . . . not computers or condominiums. A chip meant a piece of wood. Hardware meant hardware, and software wasn't even a word.

Back then, "made in Japan" meant junk, and the term "making out" referred to how you did on your exam. Pizzas, McDonald's and instant coffees were unheard of. We hit the scene when there were 5-and 10-cent stores where you bought things for five and ten cents. Larry's sold ice cream cones for a nickel or a dime. For one nickel you could ride a street car make a phone call, buy a Pepsi or buy enough stamps to mail one letter and two postcards. You could buy a new Chevy coupe for $600 . . . but who could afford one? A pity, too, because gas was only 11 cents a gallon!

In our day, grass was mowed. Coke was a cold drink and pot was something you cooked in. Rock music was a grandma's lullaby and AIDS were helpers in the Principal's office. We were certainly not before the difference between the sexes was discovered, but we were surely before the sex change. We made do with what we had. And we were the last generation that was so dumb as to think you needed a husband to have a baby. No wonder we are so confused and there is such a generation gap today. But, we survived!! What better reason to celebrate?? [Footnote: This is based on an article that has been around awhile; source unknown.]

Memories

Abe Morales • Class of 1937 • Gary, IN

Do you remember?

- Kerosene sold in grocery stores for those of us who had our electricity turned off?
- The horse water troughs on Michigan Avenue by the

Indiana Theater?

- The boys playing marbles, the girls playing hopscotch and jacks by Riley School?
- Mr. Ballard belting out "When they cut down the old pine tree" during our auditorium sessions at Riley School?
- The Rollins twins at Katherine House and also Barney Slamkowski?
- The nightly hide-and-seek games on Deodar Street by the old Nehi plant?
- The residents on Beech and Alder Streets taking their cows and goats to graze at Cline Avenue across from Columbus Drive?
- The camaraderie between the Romanians and Mexicans who lived on Block and Pennsylvania in the 1930s: Nick Hanzi, "Beans" El Mico, Dan Ben, Chuck Pumnea, Charley Vela, Jesse Villapando, Pete Puskas, Alex Vraciu, Sam Veuuvka?
- The Marathon dance contests at the old Turner Hall?

A Great Way To Pay Back an Old Bet

Margaret (Burke) Berryman • Class of 1936 •

Evansville, IN

Receiving each issue of the ANVIL is eagerly anticipated. Thanks to all of you for a wonderful gift of love for our beloved WHS. I also must thank Arliss Fuhrmark Cox, class of 1938, for sending in a donation to you in my name. She told me she was paying off an old bet she and I made in late 1945. We were both back home with our parents in Sunnyside while our husbands were in service overseas. During those lonely times we tried to console each other when those much anticipated letters were slow to arrive. Apparently the bet was: The one whose husband got home first had to take the other one out to dinner. She didn't pay off. Needless to say, I wouldn't

Now I would like to request that you send the ANVIL to Frances (Balich) and Bob Evans, both of the class of 1938. Fran is the widow of my brother, Tom Burke, class of 1921. A donation is enclosed.

Growing Up In Indiana Harbor

(From a speech given to the Class of 1936 at the 50th Reunion)

Dave Nassau • Class of 1936 • Olympia Fields, IL

Greetings one and all. About 30 years ago, Mr. Williams, father of one of the quiz kids, told me that he was traveling to Lafayette, Indiana, to attend his 50th reunion at Purdue University. I thought, "My gosh, what a milestone to reach!! Well, here we are at our 50th high school reunion and I have only four years until my 50th reunion at Purdue University.

I don't know about you folks, but I feel young and I'm certain all in attendance tonight are here to celebrate the fact that we are the youngest in spirit and zest for life of all the senior citizens in the USA.

We were there in the beginning and now at the end of good old WHS, Our grandparents and parents were pioneers in an industrial area that represents one of the last frontiers in the USA. Industrial Lake County was not developed until after 1900.

In the five decades we are celebrating, we have been through depressions, recessions, strikes and three wars. It was half a century that saw the greatest advancement in technology in the history of the world. Atomic power, space travel and scientific breakthroughs in communication and medicine. The radio to us was an unbelievable achievement. Remember the crystal sets placed between two dinner plates?

We have witnessed a lessening of the moral values that were taught to us by our teachers, many who were recruited

147

from southern Indiana by our superintendents.

We were taught thrift. Remember the pennies and nickels we took to school each week to be put in the bank? All was lost in the Depression; however, we learned to save. We were taught to revere the flag of our country, and our four-letter word was "work."

The Harbor represented the true American melting pot. Eighty nationalities were in our class. We learned tolerance and empathy and the words desire and patriotism were part and parcel to our lives. The politicians were mayors Hale, Rooney and Migas, and ruling City Hall with an iron hand was Glennette Holmes' mother.

Remember Doctors Teegarden, Mervis and Niblick? Judges Crites and Callahan? Boy Scout Executive A. Sambrook, Truant Officer Fred Busey, St. Pat's Father Pop Connelly and Bertha McQuaid, who ran the board of education?

In the business district, there was Gould's, Miller's, Tarler's Shoes, Shutan's Pharmacy, Shock's Calumet Laundry, Zimmerman's Department Store, the Barker Furniture Store, and the Interurban Restaurant of Joe Esola. Central Drug for a frostie sundae, and of course, Larry Ladella, holding forth at the Busy Corner soda fountain. The Harbor was at its zenith.

The Big House hosted by Sonny Sheets and Peck Gardner where the Wheel of Fortune spun for one and all, we were told. Taboo also was the bordello at 3311 Michigan Avenue.

Remember the ice skating rink on the south end of the old football field. Washington Park had a real live zoo, and Lake Front Beach, where we boys went swimming B.A.B.

For seven cents, one could travel to downtown Gary or Hammond on a street car, and for a bit more to Chicago.

The horse and wagon delivered our milk and ice, and the rags and iron man. The two-wheeled cart propelled by the expert scissor and knife sharpener, who for a dime would hone the edges with great precision. Mr. Huttle, with his team of

148

horses and great excavating shovel.

There were automobiles the likes of Duarnt, Essex, Hudson, Rickenbacker, Willys-Knight, Pierce Arrow, Ajax, Packard, Franklin and Studebaker. I remember one frosty winter night, Chuck Moore drove five of us to the dunes in his father's Hudson Terraplane. He was traveling 80 miles an hour on an icy road. Now you know why I'm so short; I lost three inches of height that evening from fright!

Back to the school environs, who can forget Roy and Russell Robinson, our iron-handed, but fair, principals. Coach Frank Cash, Sue Cook, Ann Cooley, Robert White and Pauline Shearer, who directed the famous Robeson Glee Club and brought music into our lives. Mr. Dickes and his future bride, Miss Jacoby, Mr. Sigler and so many more.

Remember cold winter mornings when you went out to fetch the milk and the cardboard lid was pushed up three inches by the frozen cream? The Gypsies who roamed the alleys and told fortunes to our mothers. The minstrel shows, and of course, Bank Night at the Indiana Theater. The beach parties at the dunes where we sat around the fire and sang, "I want a girl, just like the girl," "There's a long, long road a winding," "We were sailing along on a moonlit bay," and most of us were wet behind the ears. A kiss to us was ecstasy. What a wonderful time to grow to man and womanhood.

Remember the World's Fair in Chicago? We traveled back and forth by jitney cab for fifty cents a round trip.

We went through an era that produced the greatest heros in the world of sports: Babe Ruth, Hank Greenberg, Bob Feller, Ted Williams, Jack Dempsey, Big Bill Tilden and Red Grange. We had our own heros in the sports world.

Some of the people in attendance were: Hank Ford, Paul Koscar, Dr. Charles Niblick, John Laucis Backfield, Jack Siekien, Steve Bacon, Wallace Skierge and William White. Some teachers that were present were: Miss Skretny, Pinky

Harbor Memories: Summertime Coolers

Johnson, Earl Keller, Walter McCoy, Mr. Altenderfer and his wife, and John McShane.

The Bland Life

Lee Sterling • Class of 1938 • Pagosa Springs, CO

Harold Goodman's "Coincidence" dwarfs anything I ever experienced or possibly anyone else. Living in six different states and four years in the Service, I met one man from Whiting, one from East Chicago (Roosevelt '39), and a young woman from Michigan City, never met anyone I served with in Signal Corp. and no one from the Harbor—so much for my "coincidences." I would like to compete for the "Bland Life Award," if you ever offer competition. Oh yes, I did meet

Arliss Fuhrmark's delightful nephew, Tom, who resides and is a graphic artist in Durango and his dad in Plano, Texas, who was from the Harbor, so that belies my earlier remark.

Mr. Goodman's former house-boy turned American entrepreneur would make a fascinating nonfiction book. I would be the first to order it.

After leaving the class of 1938, I worked in a steel mill, Carnegie, IL, South Works while attending Northwestern Univ., Chicago Campus; a war interrupted my carefully programmed plans, and I spent about four years doing the military thing while occasionally going to places I didn't like.

I moved to California in 1946 and married Patty in 1948. We targeted moving to the mountains when we retired in 1985, which we did in 1987. Patty is a ski nut, as a matter of fact, she's in Park City, Utah, as I write. I stopped such foolishness after a slight stroke in 1997, which also stopped my flying lessons, just when the instructor was beginning to relax.

A highlight of my life was in the summer of 1989 when ten of us had a WHS mini-reunion in Durango, Colorado. It was Joe Siminski's first air travel. There was Joe, his sister, Helen, and daughter Cynthia, Marian Fedorek Laud, and Lillian "Frye" and Wally Van Kempema, Jeanne "Duffy" and Joe McGuire. As I remember, Lillian's sister Ruth had a health problem at that time and could not come. It was a great week for all and Joe was turned on to air travel.

When I tell you we've lived in California, Minnesota, Illinois and Texas—the longest and the last 14 years in Colorado, you have the story of my life. Who says short, old guys can't luck out?

Remember When

David Nassau • Class of 1936 • Olympia Fields, IL

In 1928, I was water boy for the football team coached by Frank Cash. The field the team practiced and played on was covered with cinders from Inland Steel. Also in 1928, a convict in Michigan City, Indiana, built a replica of Horse Feathers, the horse from the old Barney Goggle comic strip, and gave it to the Michigan City High School basketball team. They were to keep the horse until they were beaten. Well, East Chicago Washington beat them and they kept possession of Horse Feathers for the rest of the year, as the team went unbeaten. Before each basketball game, Horse Feathers was rolled out onto the floor amid much cheering from the crowd. I was a student manager of the football and basketball teams from 1932 to 1936 under coaches Cash and McShane. What wonderful role models they were.

Remember the fireworks each night when the Bessemer Furnace would convert iron into steel at The Youngstown Sheet & Tube Company? When the wind was right, we could smell the Chicago Stockyards and the Whiting Oil Refinery.

During the Depression, vacant stores were converted into ping pong parlors. We played for 5-cents an hour. We had a team of John Farmer, Joe Kolady and I that played teams from South Bend and Chicago. Joe Kolady became Pacific Area Ping Pong Champion during the war, and I won College Humor Magazine Ping Pong Champion at Purdue University, which gave me national ranking.

Abe's Story

Abe Morales • Class of 1937 • Gary, IN

I didn't see my name in the list of members from 1937. A lot of my classmates don't remember me, I went to the reunion and only Don Yohe knew me. Maybe it's because my buddy Earl Creekmore and I took the vocational courses. I was active in the patrol boys with Mr. Frankenhauser, and the WHS Annual Review. Vera Hedinger was also in the review; I remember from church and the christian endeavor, her brothers Wenton, Harold and Len.

When I graduated, I could not find a job, so I enrolled in the CCC, one of President Roosevelt's greatest youth programs. Our tour of duty was for two years, and the strict discipline and hard work came in handy when WWII came along and we went off to war. I served with the Marines in the South Pacific. So, you see, I was gone from the Harbor, B.A.B., the Vic and Garden Theaters, and Jim's Chili Parlor for two years in the CCC, and then three years in the Marines. No wonder no one remembered me.

My wife is a Roosevelt graduate. We married before I went into the service 58 years ago. She is a retired teacher and we have been involved in community and veterans programs for over 40 years. We have a son and a daughter, both Vietnam era army veterans.

Does anyone remember Snyders across the street from WHS? They served the greasiest, thick hamburgers that were utterly delicious!

More Memories

Ann (Vana) Livingston • Class of 1938 • Fisher, IL

Way back in memories—at the Indiana Theater, Mary Tranos worked there along with my brother, George Vana. We hung out at Larry's on Michigan Ave; I worked at Carson's Furs on Michigan Ave; the drivers would make me repeat the address 3311 Michigan when I was delivering stored or cleaned furs back to the girls. I never let on that I knew where they were picking up fur coats.

My brothers, George and John, were picked up by the Paddy Wagon for swimming in the nude, at B.A.B. (bare-ass beach). There was an old lady watching them with binoculars who reported them. What a way to get your kicks. The Public Library was a nice place to meet the boys. I lived on Broadway—was only three blocks to Lincoln, Riley and Washington Schools. Talk about location.

Thank you for the ANVIL, it is very good to read about the old days. I (We—George Vana who lives with us, and my husband Ken, who typed this letter) enjoyed the picnic. Great food, fellowship and I never saw so many OLD people!

Memories

Steve Stan • Class of 1933 • Sun City Center, FL

I wish to compliment you on the concept and the ideas you are using to pull all the people who attended WHS together. I enjoy every word in the news and am impressed with the number of celebrities who were our classmates.

When I think back to my high school days (which I do often), the most memorable time that I enjoyed was playing football.

It was a thrill to me every time I ran onto the football field to participate in a game. I loved playing football and have many wonderful memories of the people I played with and against. The climax of my football days came in 1933 when I was selected to be on the HAMMOND TIMES All-State Football Team. This team was composed of the players selected by the TIMES as the best in the state. Needless to say, I am still proud of having been a part of that tradition.

Keep the news coming. Just wish I were close enough to attend the parties and luncheons. Best Wishes to all of you.

Calumet Region
Ed Zywiec PE • Class of 1939 • Naperville, IL

I am happy to see that someone is keeping the spirit of good old WHS alive and I offer good wishes for its continued success. What bothers me is all that reference to Harborites and Da Harbor. What about the Calumet delegation? Are we the orphans and forgotten alumni? We could not afford the nickel bus fare so we had a half-hour walk through rain and sleet and snow. Although our numbers were small, we, too, are proud to be a part of WHS Alumni Assn. We did have some outstanding students and athletes from the Calumet area but at my age I can't remember their names. So how about a little recognition and a pat on the back to the Calumet area alumni?

Among my memories was Ray Robin's panel truck. Occasionally Ray would have use of the panel truck and let us know that we could ride with him. The number of riders on that small truck was amazing—bodies kept coming out just like at a circus. The number would qualify for the Guiness Book of Records.

155

Remember the Revues and School Clubs

Mattie Upshaw • Class of 1936 • Gary, IN

My heart was delighted and my memories jogged when I saw "The Washington Revue, Pauline M. Shearer, Director." She also organized the Paul Robeson Glee Club of which I was a member. I was in a couple of revues and I can never forget dancing to the Casablanca and singing "Old Man River." I spent a lot of my high school years on the WHS varsity track team. I went to the Indiana state meet and won the hundred-yard dash, placed first in the high jump and placed in the shot put. Our relay team also won.

In 1936, my dreams and aspirations were shattered when I married in my senior year and all my awards, letters, ring, emblems and sweater were destroyed or lost. I received my diploma with over a four-point average, but I didn't walk across the stage.

Since then I have completed 20 years with H&R Block. In addition, I had been a bookkeeper for 15 years for my brother's business, Tn-State Enterprise. I presently work as a caregiver.

Just Call Me Lee

Leonore Brazier Gallant • Class of 1938 • Honolulu, HI

I remember some of our classmates: Lee Sterling from elementary school days, Ione Williams, Irene Speros Herlocker Myers and Libby Tarler Irvin were my "best friends," and I still keep in touch, spending time with each when I am in the area. Both (with their husbands) have visited me here in Hawaii. I became reacquainted with Frances Balich Evans by a fluke. (Her husband worked for the Red Cross in Guam during WWII and they came to Hawaii for a little R&R) I passed her at a supermarket, nodded at this familiar face, and after she passed and said, "Lenore," I knew it was someone from Indiana Harbor from years earlier, as no one has called me "Lenore" since my school days.

For the record, my name is LEONORE. In school, teachers called me Lenore, Lorraine, Louise, etc. My sister suggested they call me "Lee" even in elementary school, but I didn't want to be called the same name as Lee Sterling. After high school, I surrendered, after the first person mangled my name I would say, "Why don't you just call me Lee."

Since legally, I am Leonore (on all my papers), that's my starting point. After 81 years, how can one's bio be brief, unless one never left home. I'll try.

After taking odd jobs, I worked for the State of Indiana Unemployment Compensation Division in Logansport, South Bend, and Da Harbor, in that order, and made good friends at each place. One such, from South Bend, married an ensign at Notre Dame, whose destroyer was based in NYC. She asked me to join her there. So I did. In NYC, I worked for the United Seaman's Service, an organization like the USO that served the merchant marine. I was lucky there and when they opened up jobs for clerks overseas, I applied and was sent to Aruba, N. A., Panama and Hawaii, arriving here September 10, 1945.

This is where my heart is. When people would ask me if I ever got homesick, my standard reply, "If you knew where I came from, you would know I'd be crazy. Why, we had smog before the word was invented." Anyway, I had four children, divorced, and at the age of 47 entered University of Hawaii, got my BA degree in Secondary Ed, English, at age 50, and later my masters. I taught English until June of 1986. I love to travel and have been to Europe several times, including Latvia, Lithuania, Belarus, Moscow and St. Petersburg. Also, Alaska, China, Japan, Australia, New Zealand, Guatamala and Costa Rica.

I am a Shakespeare nut and attend the Oregon Shakespeare Fest in Ashland, Oregon. Way back in 1973, we went across country in our Volkswagen van. I have four children, eight grandchildren and two great-grandchildren. Here I am centrally located and am into oil painting, t-shirt painting, and have season tickets for the symphony, opera and various community theaters. Over the years, I have volunteered for various charitable organizations.

From Pagoda Springs, Colorado
Lee Sterling • Class of 1938 • Pagosa Springs, CO

Recently I phoned my dear friend Joe Siminski for a street name so I could relate an incident that happened at the A&P while I was attending WHS. I innocently asked if he would get a copy of the street map common in local phone books. Subsequently I was called by Frank Hanak who gave me the street name during a wonderful phone visit. I have long been used to Joe's faithfulness to an old buddy by telling Frank about a friend in need.

I had forgotten about Joe's unparallel humor and was not prepared for the 3x4-ft. blue print map of the Harbor I received shortly after.

The A&P story is forgotten. I wish I was younger just so I'd have more time to recall Joe's friendship along with Paul Stimson's. We walked many miles together. As I look through our 1938 ANVIL, every face represents the most formative period of my character. They are all precious.

Incidentally, we have perfect blue skies, 80-degree days and 40-degree nights. Two problems, we are in a serious drought and in constant fear of fires. Don't you think wine was invented to help give us the courage we need?

George Hanzi, Sophie Ranich,
Class of 1941, attired for
Hobo Day.

Frank E. Gilbert

Hobo Day or Bum Day

Phillip A. Gilbert • Class of 1942 • Tacoma, WA

Dear Frank, I've enclosed this picture of my brother, Frank E. Gilbert, class of 1939. He's outfitted himself for senior class "Bum Day."

Perhaps you knew him? This is in response for historical (hysterical) pictures for the pamphlet you're compiling. We lived at 3814 Deodar Street, the same block as Katherine House and two doors from Bob and Ray Krajewski. [Editor's Note: Later in the 40's we called it "Hobo Day." We wonder when it changed.]

Class of 1939, ?, Joe Sarengach, John Elish

Joe Sarengach ('39), Barrey Jordan ('37), Tony Ancich ('39)

CHAPTER NINE
9
Memories From the 1940s

In April, 1945, President Franklin Roosevelt died, and he was succeeded by Vice President Harry Truman. World War II finally ended. There was no minimum wage, and life expectancy was 62.9 years. The atom bomb was invented; as were frozen meals, Tupperware and streptomycin.

The best picture of the year was "Lost Week-End," for which Ray Milland received the Oscar. Joan Crawford was best actress for her role in "Mildred Pierce."

Other pictures of note from that decade were: "Citizen Kane," "The Bank Dick," "Children of Paradise," "Dance, Girl, Dance," "Double Indemnity," "The Maltese Falcon," "Open City" and "The Palm Beach Story."

Some of the popular songs of that decade were: "April in Paris," "Cold, Cold, Heart," "I Love You for Sentimental Reasons," "Get Me to the Church on Time," "Getting to Know you," "The Happy Wanderer," "Luck Be a Lady," "Memories Are Made of This," "No Other Love," "Stranger in Paradise" and "Till There Was You."

Other interesting data from that year:

Average income	**$2,390.00**
New car	**$1,025.00**
New house	**$4,625.00**
Loaf of bread	**$0.09**
Gallon of gas	**$0.15**
Gallon of milk	**$0.62**
Gold, per oz	**$35.00**
Silver, per oz	**$0.71**
Dow-Jones avg.	**169.00**

The Unforgettable First Day

Michael Arsulich • Class of 1946 • San Diego, CA

As a naive, new sophomore student to the campus of WHS, I arrived early to obtain my class schedule. My classes were set well in advance from my previous school, Garfield Elementary. I assured my parents that I would never skip class and would be a good student.

Finding the first class was easy. We were alphabetically grouped by class and sex. A through D was our section. Notes were read that specified that all students had five minutes to get to their next class, to be seated, pencils sharpened and textbooks opened to the proper page. We were told that any tardiness would be penalized with one after-school detention.

Leaving Mr. Foster's class the first day was bedlam. Approaching an upper classman, I asked, "Where is room 203?" "203!" he replied. "That's easy, you know that building on the other side of the campus? Just go in there and walk upstairs."

"Thank you," I replied. A female teacher in the hallway of Washington Elementary told me that there was no room 203 in that building. I should proceed to the building on the north side of the high school campus and go to the second floor. I was late. After my first class, we rushed out of the room so fast, I didn't ask for directions to the metal shop.

Another upperclassman indicated the metal shop to be on the east side of the campus. Entering the huge door, I looked left and right. While walking upstairs, I had an uneasy feeling that this site didn't seem quite right. The stairs led me to a gymnasium with a huge balcony. This did not look like a metal shop to me! Mr. Schweingruber spotted my bewilderment. He sent me with all dispatch to Mr. Saboff's metal shop class.

By now I was becoming oriented with the campus. I was told that there was a grace period for lateness the first day of school. Thank goodness! Those damn upperclassmen! I chose to ask the wrong ones! What a welcome!

Mary Ann (Boldi) Gotch • Class of 1946 • Nipomo, CA

The new ANVIL is great. The stories from the early alumni are fun to read. There was so much talent that came out of the Harbor and we were fortunate to have such good teachers, parents and grandparents who instilled pride and hard work in their children.

I am in touch with classmates Sylvia (Fleisher) Stephens, Marilyn (Johnson) Loar, Irene (HIad) Mosny, Joe and Mary (Gaio) Cabeen, Pat (John) Grdinich, Margaret (Christoff) Brewer and Malvina (Bartok) Zampino ('45). Mal was my maid of honor.

Violet (Chulay) Manuszak ('45) lives 35-40 miles away and she keeps me up-to-date on news from home. Lillian (Melchoire) Swift and Wanda (McKeethan) Woods are just a few miles away.

One thing I don't miss from home is the snow turning dirty and black because it couldn't melt fast enough.

Deja Vu All Over Again

Bob Krajewski • Class of 1944 • Munster, IN

"My first official visit to WHS in March, 1950, as a new East Chicago Public School teacher certainly was a case of deja vu for me. All the sights, sounds and even the smells of WHS which I left as a student in June, 1946, came back in a familiar rush.

Here I was walking the halls between classes and I didn't even need a pass! No hall monitor bugged me; after all, I

163

was wearing a shirt and tie. Strictly speaking, I wasn't a classroom teacher, I was an itinerant speech and hearing therapist working with communication-handicapped students individually or in smalgroups. The current title for this group is speech and language pathologist.

An interesting aspect of my new professional status was the query of several building clerks who knew me well, "Do I have to call you Mr. Krajewski, or is Bob still OK?"

Since I was now part of the gang, the previous somewhat distant student-teacher relationships became warmer, so Mr. Kincaid was now Pete, Mr. Palmer was Charley, Miss Sufana became Mary, Mr. Schweingruber became "Dutch," Mr. Clark had always been "Potsy."

However, in my mind, others remained as they always had been internalized by me, for example: Mr. Dickes, Mr. Souter, Miss Boomer. After all, who could say "Hi, Nellie" to Miss Mills?

In that 1950-52 era, there were a few rather recent WHS grads who were newly minted teachers. Without researching, the following come to mind: Jo Babas, Paul Barkal, Paul and Mike Guiden, Ray Krajewski, Betty Lou Oberg and Jules Siegle. (Those I've omitted may contact the editor.) Perhaps they all had similar nostalgic feelings at their first professional day at WHS.

It's only a personal observation; not backed by any surveys, but I believe a larger than expected percentage of WHS grads of the 1942-50 era went into education. Part of this press came from a sense of service, a desire for education that led into teaching, but much of it, I believe, came from a nostalgic review of the pleasant supportive and encouraging atmosphere they encountered at Washington.

Top Row (L to R): Sherrie Nathanson Friedman, Rose Goodmen Selesnick, Larraine Kirilova, Helen Kosavac Kovac, Maggie Michaels, Ruth Brenman Baker. Bottom Row: Liz Dragoin Lemon, Aldona Kesilis, Inez Levin Abrahamson, Kathy (?), Louise Forsberg Lucas. All of the above are from the class of 1944 except Inez Levin Abrahamson, who is a 1946 alum.

1947 Highlights

From Florida

Georgette Walsh Diaz • Class of 1949 • Melbourne, FL

The picnic in August must have been great; I'm sorry I missed it. Since I sold my condo in Schererville in October, 1999, Melbourne, FL, is now my permanent home. I started attending Washington in fourth grade, having come from Lincoln School, and graduated in 1949. There were many wonderful teachers; Miss Sufana, Miss Boomer and Mr. Brunswick, just to mention a few. I have many fond memories of the Harbor, growing up on the 38th block of Ivy Street. Oh, yes! Hanak's Bakery just around the corner, with it's wonderful, fragrant goodies. Going to football games at Roosevelt, then walking back to Larry's for sodas and cokes.

I also enjoyed reading Archibald McKinlay's book about "Da Regin" that he autographed for me at the Awards dinner last year. The ANVIL is a great idea! I enjoy the letters people write about their memories and recollections of the Region and WHS. Bob Krajewski's column was hilarious in the July, 2000 issue. Through the years, I have actually heard some of those expressions and comments. In fact, my husband, Peter, wanted to know why I was chuckling so much. Keep it up Bob. I do have one regret, that I wasn't able to participate in after-school activities because of my responsibilities at home, which included looking after my younger brother.

After graduation from WHS and while working at Inland Steel, I met and married Ed Walsh, with whom I had three lovely daughters. Ed passed away 19 years ago after 30 wonderful years of marriage. My daughters are: Georgette Walsh Goodwin, married to a corporate attorney for Bechtel Corp.; they have three children, two sons ages 16 and 13 and a 9-year-old daughter. Katherine Walsh Ryan, married to an Indianapolis physician who specializes in endocrinology and hormonal disorders; they have a 6-year-old son. Nora Walsh

Dalgado, married and both she and her husband work for S.B. A. in Edmond, OK; they have a 2-year-old daughter. While visiting a friend in Florida, I met my present husband, Peter Diaz, a retired Air Force Major. We have now been married for six years.

Among his hobbies, Peter loves to travel. We have traveled throughout the U.S. We went to China, walked the Great Wall, visited the Forbidden City and cruised the Yangtze River. Shanghai is a fascinating city. We then visited Hong Kong, a breathtaking city. Two years later, we spent a month in Australia and New Zealand. A must see! Last year we visited Romania and met my relatives. It was a wonderful and very emotional experience. A month later we visited London, then on to Luxembourg and Germany. Next we visited Vienna, Venice, Zurich and Paris, all by train. We truly love Europe and plan to go back to visit many other countries.

My First Prom

Jack Culver • Class of 1946 • Crown Point, IN

It was in my sophomore year—a great year—running the 1/2-mile (dead man's run) with Richard Gonzales and Wendell Campbell. They had longer legs so I was always in third place. Then came football—made the first string varsity and played left guard next to Cordovers Tucker (tackle). What a pair we were, And the guys we played across from us knew we were there.

Then came prom time. I was asked by an upper class-woman. It was a big surprise for me. She asked me so late there wasn't time to rent a tux. So I wore a light-tan suit. It was also too late to double up with someone in a car. Cars were pretty scarce then. My mom had her Twin City Floral delivery truck, but I opted to use a "cab." I think that was a first for WHS.

I figured that at the dance we could get a ride to go out afterwards—Chicago, Wells Street Beach, etc. Not a chance. Those upperclassmen didn't want little 'o' me and my date ride'n with them.

So, she and I (in her formal) walked to the "Grill" (Broadway and Main Street). She had shrimp, I had pork chops. I'm sure this experience is never forgotten. Walking back to her home, we slipped into a back seat of a car and had our good-night smooches. I bet we had more fun than the Chicago bunch.

Fishing Lake Michigan

Richard Rudzinski • Class of 1943 • Munster, IN

I was bitten by the "fishin' bug" early in life. By the time I had enrolled in Washington High, my buddies and I had a full-blown case of the "fishin' fever" surging through our veins.

Lake Michigan was our "fishin' hole." Tasty yellow perch and fresh-water herring was what we were after. A bunch of us hung around with each other. We came from east of Main Street, south of Broadway and north of Columbus Drive. We didn't particularly care for our given names. Fayo, Drake, Duke, Etchka, Tuba, Fats, Tuffy and Spike were but some of what we called each other. Most, if not all of us, graduated from "Bonehead College," St. John Cantius School.

We would scrounge the alleys, basements and attics for paper, bottles and scrap to sell to the "junk man" for a few pennies. Enough to go to Miss Stacia Skrentny's brother's hardware store in the 3900 block of Main Street to purchase the needed tackle, a long cane pole, a short length of cat gut, a lead sinker and some cutty hunk line. Lake Michigan shiners were the bait of choice. The water was teeming with thousands of little emerald shiners whose silver sides flashed like diamonds as they swam. An old lace curtain with two old broom handles became an excellent seine to capture the bait. We

168

knew Indiana Harbor like the backs of our hands, all the short cuts were familiar. A hole through the Universal Atlas Cement property fence and across the railroad tracks was a secluded little beach near Buffington Pier—B.A.B., "Best American Beach," if you prefer.

Upon arrival we'd strip down to our birthday suits, swim awhile, seine some shiners and amble over to Buffington Pier. It was no problem catching a hundred or more perch in those glory days.

One particular day looms large in my memory. A beautiful Indian Summer day, the lure of B.A.B. and fishing was stronger than the toll of the school bell. We granted ourselves a self-proclaimed holiday. It was fun for awhile, but it didn't last. We swam, got the bait and went to dress to go fishing. Guess who was sitting on our neatly piled clothes? There was an old two-wheeled bike in the scene. You guessed it! Old Mr. Busse, the truant officer. How in hell did he find us? How in hell could he get there on a two-wheeled bike? We'll never know. For me it was the last time to play hookey and go fishing. Then came the time in our lives when a little black-haired jerk sporting a little black mustache and his little Emperor buddy from across the other side of the world really screwed things up.

Fishin' fever had been pre-empted by a patriotic fever . . . a number of us from the classes of 1942 and 1943 wanted to graduate early and join the fray. When it ended, many did not return. Those of us who were lucky enough, came back to Indiana Harbor. We saw the same steel mills, the same school, alleys and neighborhoods. Things appeared the same, but they were different. It was not the same old Harbor anymore!

George Hanzi, Sophie Ranich, Class of 1941, attired for Hobo Day.

Class of 1941 SENIOR ANVIL Signing Day for John Hanak and Sophie Ranich.

Some of the regulars at Dino's Sweet Shop, corner of 149th and Main Street (L to R) Jim Tracey, class of 1951, Dino, Phil Tracey, Class of 1951, Clark Wilson, Class of 1952.

Sophie Ranich, Cy Gillespie and May Golish enjoy a 1941 beach party.

The Decca Club (1945)

Back Row (L to R): Malvina (Bartok) Zampino, Wini (Gaither) Ratajczak, Hana (Chobanov) Ralish, Eva Adel (Schlossberg) Cohen, Esther Spector, Geri (Dolnics) Wargin.
Front Row (L to R): Dorothy (LaBanc) Mendyke, Barbara (East) Saunders, Gayle (Tolf) Farmer, Dorothy (Smith) Cameron.

Arizona Recall

Faye Freidland Hein • Class of 1940 • Phoenix, AZ

The ANVIL that is sent to me refreshes my very "old" memory.

- The Garden Theater was oh so great. While waiting in line for the movie, you collected a glass plate.
- The ice cream at Larry's—the best in days of yore. My friends and I would gather there for gossip and to explore.
- The Indiana Theater featured "top stars" for just a dime. Three times a week we'd view the film and have a wonderful time.
- I'm glad I was born in 1922 and revered the world with respect. My parents demanded courtesy and honesty thoughts reflect.
- The days at WHS were spent on mastering every course. The teachers did their very best with bonding and no remorse.
- "Kudos" to you, Frank, Ed and staff. You have the ability to bring forth some tears and a laugh.
- Oh I loved the Indiana Harbor. I thought it so "sporty." It was a thrill for me to graduate in "good old 1940."
- To all the graduates of Washington High. You're the best; I admire like "apple pie."

Living on Euclid Avenue

Jim Potesta • Class of 1941 • East Chicago, IN

While growing up in the Harbor, I think of the years I spent living in the 141st block of Euclid Ave. This was a densely populated block due to the many multiple-family dwellings.

As I look back, I can remember where each family lived and the names of most of the kids that became WHS graduates. It was a block of diverse nationalities and religions.

Living on the east side of Euclid were Virginia, Tony and Yvonne Puchely; Joe, Tony, Jim, Mary and Carmela Zajejcia; Barbara and Matthew Matczynski; Edward, Lois and Jim Martell; Howard, Dick and Jim Holland; David (Yosh), Annette and Ruth Brenman; Clara, Vicki, Bob, Norbert and Victoria Delnick; Phillip, Harold and Bob Goodman, who married the very pretty Dana Parducci of the Busy Corner Parduccis. Continuing on to Evelyn, Rose and Martin Goodman, cousins to the other Goodman family; Morton, Dorothy, Bob and George Turbow; Leon, Pearl and Kenneth Goldberg; Vince Boryla, noted sports figure, businessman and philanthropist.

Living on the west side of Euclid were Bob and Lorraine Lind; John, Edward and Helen Kipta; Harry Snedden; Douglas and Sam Clark; Charles Moore; Mary, Ann, John and Christine Sukupchak; Dan and Mary Adeline Frankenhouser. Around the corner on Columbus Drive as we extend Euclid to include Ray and Edward Regalis.

I feel ever so gratefl ul sharing mutual respect and great camaraderie with all the members of the 141st block of Euclid Avenue.

Coincidences

Harold F Goodman • Class of 1942 • Los Angeles, CA

I once edited my fishing club's newsletter and know how tough it is to get a flow of contributions. Competition helps. Letters to the ANVIL must necessarily be weighted to autobiography and that's how it should be. However, it occurs to me that a unique approach in your infant publication might be a feature titled "Coincidences." I have heard numerous stories from friends who'd run into total strangers in the most unexpected places and learn that they'd lived next door to each other years earlier. Indiana Harbor was sometimes the link. Who hasn't been involved in coincidences? Those stories can be amusing, breath-taking, entertaining, etc. An annual prize, such as a WHS polo shirt, might be offered to the winner. The decision of the judges would be final; there would be no limit on entries, etc. Duplicate lies could be easily detected.

Here is my favorite hair-raiser and it is true: My wife is, among other things, a jazz nut. For years we would spend a long weekend at the Monterey Jazz Festival. About fifteen years ago, we decided to go into Carmel for an early dinner before the evening concert. I spotted a sign: Manchurian Chinese Restaurant. We decided to try it. Very nicely done. We were the first patrons and went to the bar. The owner came out and decided to serve us. He was in his late thirties, wore an elegant suit, and spoke excellent, accented English.

I said, "Manchurian Chinese restaurant. We've never known one before."

"Would you like to hear the story?"

"Yes."

"I was orphaned in a small town in North China during the Japanese occupation. When the American military came in after the war, I got a job with them. They adopted me, sent me to the States where I was educated, got a bachelor's at Harvard and a master's at Harvard Business School, then decided to open a Manchurian restaurant in Carmel. We're doing very well."

I was thinking to myself, "American military? North China? Small town?"

"What was the name of that town?"

"Oh, you'd never have heard of it."

"Taku-Bar?" I said.

His eyes lit up. "You were a marine."

"No. I was a navy corpsman attached to the Marines."

"Then you were in the dispensary?"

"Yes."

"Where was your room?" he asked.

"There was a corridor behind the dispensary. I had the

first room on the left."

The assault battalion was out there to occupy an abandoned Japanese cavalry outfit and guard a huge military dump that both Chiang Kai Shek and Mao Tse Tung were eyeing. We came from Okinawa.

I remembered the child who polished my boots, made up the bunk and shaved me in the morning for a nickel. The connection was made in about the time it took you to read this.

Ice Skating at WHS

George Elish • Class of 1943 • Highland, IN

I remember when the WHS tennis courts were flooded for ice skating. They also opened the hot house to warm up. Besides skating around, some of the games we played were: "Crack the Whip," "I Got It" and "Train." To show off, we'd skate backwards.

When the guys wanted to get a girl's attention, they'd skate behind the girl and nudged the back of her knees to cause her to fall backwards into their arms. It was a neat thing, and it worked!

A personal experience occurred one wintry night. After skating for awhile, a classmate informed me that my left ear was "stiff as a board." I vividly recall that moment, although I don't remember the girl's name. The guys usually skated without hats, because it was considered "macho."

I quickly changed, and headed for my aunt's house on Euclid Avenue. No way was I going home with a frozen ear! Besides, her house was closer to the school than mine. She instructed me to gently apply warm water to it. Eventually, it "thawed." Then I headed home.

The following morning, I visited our school nurse, Miss Lonquist. She applied some salve, and informed me that my ear was OK, although it would peel. From then on, whenever I skated, I wore a hat.

Harbor Theaters

Vince Mroz • Class of 1941• Naples, FL

In the latest issue of the ANVIL, there was mention of the Indiana Theater in the Harbor. That brought back memories of what we used to do in our young days. Whenever a carnival came to town and they had left, we went around the grounds picking up the whole tickets left behind. The tickets were sorted by color and placed in cigar boxes. There were five theaters in the Harbor: the Vic, American, Garden, Broadway and Indiana. On weekends, we found out what color tickets the respective theater was issuing. We picked out what show we wanted to see. We waited for a group to enter the theater, and we went with them, handing the ticket-taker the same colored ticket upside down, and took a seat immediately. At that time, the price of a ticket was 15 to 25 cents. At the Garden Theater, you would see three movies, two cartoons and a newsreel. On Wednesday or Thursday, the Garden Theater had Ladies Day. For the price of a ticket, they would get a piece of dinnerware. I remember my sisters going every week until they completed a dinner set for four persons.

While in grade school (Riley), I was a school Patrol Boy. Every Saturday, the school patrol was admitted free to the Indiana Theater. Before the movie, the organist played songs that were put on the screen with a bouncing ball and we sang our lungs out. You had to wear your patrol belt and it had to be clean. If it was dirty, you were denied permission to enter. Every Friday night, I would scrub my patrol belt with Dutch Cleanser with a brush. It was pure white.

Mayor's Cabinet (1945)

Front Row (L to R): D. Dahlin, D. Wiersbe, N. Goodman, W. Gaither. Row 2: J. Platis, S. Cvitkovich, J. Sternberg. Row 3: Mr. Palmer, E. Misewicz, R. Goodman, J. Plesha. Row 4: J. Hlad, J. Miskovich. Row 5: C. Dahlin, A. McKinlay, F. Corban, R Hurt.

What's That Again?

Bob Krajewski • Class of 1946 • Munster, IN

Precision in language is important in any profession, and certainly no less in education. Throughout my career in administration I was extremely careful to say or write exactly what I intended: To do otherwise could result in embarrassment, ridicule or, at the worst, legal action. The other side of the coin is that I trained myself to be an active listener; I listened very carefully to what others said. As a result, I gathered a compendium of garbled oral communication: mixed metaphors, twisted adages, and words and phrases just off the mark.

And these oral goofs came from a *criss cross*, I mean cross section of employee groups and the community. It would be foolish, for example, to point to only the clerical crew because I had the responsibility to *moltivate* all employees to do better. And don't try to *pin me to the corner* to identify the worst group. The *klux* of these errors, suggested one colleague, was too much watching of their *Westemhouse* TV.

Many of the richest of these comments are within a medical or personal health framework. Understandable, because, after the latest office gossip and exaggerations of the kid's and grandkid's achievements, what is left is health-related.

One of our people had surgery on his *prostitution* gland. His wife was on her way to the pharmacy to get a *subscription* for him. He thought he might have to take two *capizes* before each meal.

Another employee who was severely disciplined was upset because the principal "rubbed salt in my *womb*."

"Sorry to hear about your dad. Was he senile?" asked a friend.

"No, his eyes were OK. He could see real good right up until the end." School board members had name plates for

178

identification at public meetings. I had to make a *diaphragm* of the seating arrangements for a new custodian.

During a heated board discussion, one of our patrons asked if he would be allowed to *dilate* (digress) on that point. Angrily, a citizen challenged the board, "You better shape up or *shake* out!" One of our gang was out ill for a long time. I heard he was in the hospital; he was in *insulation*. Understandable, because he was always *acceptable* to colds. In fact, he was so ill they had to give him *novenas* in the arm.

The entire staff at one of the schools had agreed on a dress code, and the principal was informing the PTA. He told them he was personally going to make certain that none of the girls were wearing pants.

School board meetings were often public entertainment, and the media usually performed its good works on us. In fact, they often took *pop* shots at us, according to a prejudiced observer. I had been counseled, though, never to *kow pow* to an editorial writer. Sometimes people *thump* their noses at our building or curricular plans. Some critics say there is nothing there you can really put your *handle* on. Once it was charged a new venture was going to put a *wrench in the monkey works*. Give them a chance, pleaded a friend, perhaps the plan will work out as soon as they *wrinkle the bugs out*.

One of our guys said he is tired of reading those *prefabricated* stories in the newspaper; they just stick in his *crawl*. Some of those stories use a lot of *scuttleback*. But, again, newspaper persons are a different *brood* than they were years ago.

We worked hard to clear up any misconceptions of any of our programs. So, an administrator in charge spoke publically, "Some of the people in this community have a *misdemeanor* about our transportation system."

I offered a solution during one of our perennial budget crises, but was rebuffed by one of our advisors, "You can't do that; you're barking up a *dead* tree."

We tried to hire the best teachers we could find. Our *personality* department *scoured* the Midwest; we always made certain we had a letter of *accommodation* for each applicant.

A principal reported one of the clerks had resigned notwithstanding a recent raise. The young lady told him the money was OK, but the low level job challenges were *stumping* her growth.

Perhaps it was all worthwhile, because one of the fellows said, "Well, it must be nice being the head *poncho* and having the *zinc* truck deliver your check.

Duke Ellington's 100th Birthday

Gerald Wenzel • Class of 1947 • Chesterton, IN

I rubbed shoulders with a genius, albeit one for one night. I'm speaking of Duke Ellington, the famous bandleader.

During the fifties, it was common for several big name bands to tour the armed service bases and colleges. The base where I was stationed at the time was Camp Lejeune, NC. Although this article will be about Ellington, I would like to first make some of our younger readers aware of how things were during that time at Camp Lejeune. This should help clarify a few things.

Every man who has served in the armed services will sooner or later find himself at some place he doesn't want to be. This goes with the territory. Well, Camp Lejeune is one of those places.

At Camp Lejeune, there were no flies, mosquitoes or birds. Why? Because every night, the entire area was sprayed with DDT. This killed off the bugs, birds and probably a few marines too. I can still smell the stuff. Now that this is said, I can get back to Duke Ellington and his band.

The band put on two shows, one for the enlisted men and one for the officers. I was an officer.

I was outside in the swimming pool when Duke Ellington and his band came in and started setting up for the night's festivities. One of my friends said that one of the band members was from Indiana Harbor. Naturally, I thought he was joking, and I had no intentions of attending the performance, as I didn't care about jazz, not then, not now, not ever.

I eventually went and saw them play, and sure enough, his trumpet player was Willie Cook from the Harbor. He had gone to WHS. He was in his early thirties at the time and had lived on Guthrie Street. We talked until about 1:00 am, and they had to pick up their instruments and get on the bus for the next gig.

They had a new air-conditioned bus, but there is nothing like a nice bed and shower after a hard, hot day. I asked my new friend if they could stay at our BOQ (Bachelor Officer Quarters). We got the OK, so everyone got beds.

Duke was in his fifties at the time, and his band was in their thirties. He was a nice guy, but did not get close to his band members. Duke Ellington was an imposing figure of about 6'3" and about 250 pounds—big at that time, but very soft-spoken.

He refused to bunk with his band, so I told him to come down to my room where there was an extra bed. He figured I wasn't an autograph hound and wouldn't bother him. He appreciated our hospitality before leaving, and did autograph a few pictures for me. He signed them "to my old friend Jerry," which was a stretch of the imagination, but I figured it would impress my friends back in Indiana Harbor anyway.

To my dismay, the people back home didn't give a rat's rump about Duke Ellington, Duke Wayne or Duke Farouk. So much for the autographed pictures!

Times Have Changed

Harold Goodman • Class of 1942 • Los Angeles, CA

Do you remember the fountain pen? They used to have rubber bladders inside to hold the ink. The rubber bladder manufacturers must have gone out of business with the advent of ballpoints.

The old joke has disappeared. Every Bar Mitzvah boy got a fountain pen. He was so uptight when giving his speech to the congregation with the gifts awaiting that instead of saying "Today I am a man," he said, "Today I am a fountain pen."

Do you remember the ink pen nib? We were supposed to suck on them before inserting into the slot. That was intended to remove the oil. No matter how thoroughly I did it, the ink would not stay on after dipping it in the bottle. Or, if some did stay on, it would become a blob on the paper. I never turned in a neat exercise.

In my row of 0's, no two ever matched, even between the lines. My handwriting has gotten even lousier. That's why I use a typewriter. I had many calls from pharmacists who couldn't read my prescriptions. One of them called because I got the dosage wrong, he said, "Are you trying to kill the patient?"

That's one of the reasons I retired. Also, it got so if the telephone at home rang after 7 pm I was so annoyed before picking it up. It was probably some d****d nurse asking if she could give her patient an enema.

Not Class of 1941

Dr. Mike Gordon • Class of 1942 • Lorida, FL

I was very happy to receive your informative enclosures and it revived some "Club Society" good old Parrish Avenue memories. It seems like our numbers are slowly diminishing and that is always a sadness that is inevitable.

I'm sorry, but I simply cannot recall who Ed Styles (Styberski) is or was, but he certainly has made a mark in this world. What a gift to be master of the English language and be able to express oneself as expertly as he seems to do.

I enjoyed the verbiage of my classmate Harold Goodman. The memory of the first and only birthday party I ever attended was at Harold's house. I think he lived on Carey or Drummond Street. What I remember was the milk bottle game (not spin the bottle) in which your object was to see how many clothes pins you could drop into the milk bottle, which was played at your side. I won! I don't recall, a candy bar or something similar? As I dusted off my SENIOR ANVIL to renew my memory of some of my classmates, I noticed that George Goveiah, Harold Goodman and myself were side by side—two dentists and one medical doctor—I thought that was ironic. And as I chuckled at the good luck messages scribbled in the ANVIL I came across those momentous words, "To a number one schmuk," signed by my friend Harold. Oh! Such memories. I just wonder if he can remember that great note of confidence!

But, I really would like to complement you as so many others have on the great job that you have done in and with the monthly "WEEKLY ANVIL." It's just fun and I look forward to reading about all the former students—even those that I don't know! The other day, I looked up a picture Eleanor and I had taken with Vince Mroz when we vacationed in Washington, DC. As I put my right arm around him, I could feel the holstered gun under his coat. I felt very protected. This must have been 40-45 years ago!

I don't know why or how my friend M. Martini lists my graduation as "41." That was when my brother Mitch graduated. Straighten him out please!

The ISU class reunion is on the 29th and I'm really sorry I cannot attend. I have plans for New Orleans and it is impossible to attend both places, but you can keep me informed as to what happened at the gala occasion. I would like to see the football buddies, and the great basketball players that are my friends.

Coming Home to the Harbor

George Germek • Class of 1945 • Valencia, CA

I'm writing this letter because I wanted to make some comments after reading the ANVIL, April 15, 1999, issue. My wife and I moved to California 15 years ago, and reading the article "Keeping the Memories Alive" sure brought back a lot of them.

One visit back "home" I drove to the Harbor "Region." As I drove down Columbus Drive, I kept remembering good times and good friends—playing for the school dances, singing in the chorus, growing upon Deodar Street. I drove down that street and was surprised to see my home was boarded up, and although the town had changed, I was still seeing it through the eyes of my 12-year-old self. I was remembering a church on the corner of Deodar and 139th Street. My friends and I would sit out front and about 11:30 pm Mr. Robinson would bring out some ribs that they made in the church kitchen. Another great memory is Katherine House, where we learned sports and games, but more importantly, how to get along with our neighbors.

In those days, you could buy a 5-cent ice cream cone, pay 11 cents a gallon for gas and it cost 15 cents to see a movie. All this and Lake Michigan, too—to say nothing of B. A.B. where we waved at the girls sitting on the pier with their binoculars, while we were trunkless.

Needless to say, I could go on because the article just started the memories flowing—but they are all good ones and the sad thing is that we really cannot go "home" again.

Memories from Michigan

Bill Corder • Class of 1945 • Ada, MI

I just received my ANVIL, and as usual it brought back lots of memories. First of all, regarding nicknames . . . I was known as "Two Bits" because my last name sounded like "quarter." This nickname was given to me (as best I can remember) in first grade. Bob Pastrick was known as "Pinky." Garland Chriswell was known as "Squirrel." Can't think of any more right now.

Oh, how I remember the State Champion Basketball Team in 1960. We were living in Indianapolis at the time. I was production manager of Channel 13, and my son was born in January of that year. We watched the entire game on TV, because at the time we didn't have a window to throw it out of let alone a pot to put it in. The Senators won and there was lots of bragging on my part at work. After all, that's where I went to school.

I was in the service in 1946-48. The last place I was stationed was at Fort Lawton in Seattle. I filled in one night in the dance band. As I remember, I was fourth trumpet out of four trumpets. But, the first trumpet was played by a fellow named Pete Candoli. How he could play! He went on to be a big star with some of the great bands. After the service, I majored in music at Indiana University. Finally, I realized that I would probably end up as a high school band instructor, so I transferred to Macalester College in St. Paul, MN, and took a degree in theater and a minor in music. I served as a member of the board of directors of the West Michigan Jazz Society for a time. Macalester College is where I met my lovely wife.

In June we will have been married 46 years, and we have two wonderful children. We just had our first grandchildren last June—twins, a boy and a girl. My son, who is now 40. said, "That's it Dad!"

I often think back on my days at WHS. I still keep in touch with Harry Wilber Clark, Garland Chriswell, Bill Berg and Barbara (East) Saunders. If everything works out, we will be at the 1945 Class Reunion!

Growing Up In The Harbor

Loretta (Shep) Young • Class of 1946 • Calabasas, CA

When I look back, it seems like only a short time ago that I was leading "Hail Noble Washington" with my cheerleading teammates, Sylvia (Kuzman) Kuta, Goldie (Mate) White, Lorraine Kirolova, Maggie Michaels and Sylvia Simone. What fun we had at all the games! Then, on to Ball State where I led the Cardinal fans to a different tune. Where have the years gone!

It was 1943, the beginning of my sophomore year at WHS and the first day back to school after summer vacation. My Social Science teacher, I can't remember her name, called me "Lottie" during roll call—who's Lottie? My name is Loretta, and I went by my middle name, June, all through high school.

So then, she said to the class, "Lottie's family, the Sherpetoskys, were among the first settlers in the Harbor." Wow! I could hardly wait to go home to tell my parents. They weren't impressed, no news to them. Why hadn't I been told this fascinating fact during my childhood? More important things to think about back then, I guess, like making it through the depression.

Like the rest of you, I grew up with the sights, sounds and smells of the steel mills, oil refineries, forging plants, train whistles, foghorns off Lake Michigan—and, who could forget the cries, "Ice Man" or "Rag Man," coming from the horse-driven wagons as they moved slowly through the streets and alleys.

Grandma Sherpetosky, a Lithuanian immigrant who spoke no English, ran a small grocery store in the apartment building that she and Grandpa owned on Deodar Street. Everyone in the neighborhood called her "Grandma." "Sherpetosky School of Dance" was next to the store and I, with my family, lived in an apartment above the dance studio. Grandma rented rooms in the basement to immigrants who worked in the steel mills, In retrospect, my guess is, she was also into bootlegging liquor. On occasion, I would see her take a bottle from under her apron and hand it down to someone in the basement.

Aunt Tinie, my Dad's sister, started the dancing school, but it wasn't long before her gypsy ways took over and she was off to Spain to twirl her skirts and dance to the clicking sounds of her castanets. Then on to Moscow, where she danced with the "Ballet Russe Monte Carlo." She was the first "hippie" I ever knew—a cross between that and an "Auntie Mame." She always wore a scarf around her head, gypsy fashion, lots of beads, and dressed in outlandish clothes—mostly sheer, airy-type fabrics that moved with the slightest breeze. She was carefree and happy, had an exuberant personality and a free-spirited nature. And, always in tow were her two Pekingese dogs. (Her picture appears in Archibald McKinlay's book.) How she carried off her uninhibited lifestyle while being married to an Inland Steel executive, Jim Peters, I'll never understand. Jim invented something having to do with the blast furnace at Inland.

Aunt Bessie took over the dancing school after her sister, Tinie, left for Spain. Bessie was an extremely attractive

187

woman with expensive tastes. As a child, I remember being so impressed by her full-length mink coat. She dated Martin Zarkovich, who was Chief of Detectives in the Harbor at that time. They went together for sooooo many years it seemed only natural that my sisters and I call him "Uncle Martin." However, they never married. Martin was one of the detectives who shot and killed John Dillinger as he was leaving a Chicago theater with his lady friend. The story is well known.

My father owned "Shep's Auto Body Shop" on Guthrie Street. He did all the car repairs for the Harbor Police Department; but, I clearly recall one time when he showed us a check in payment of car repairs signed by none other than "John Dillinger." We were all duly impressed because of his horrific notoriety.

My career has been with one company through the years, though there have been several company name changes due to mergers and acquisitions. First it was Rocketdyne, a division of North American Aviation, then Rockwell International, and now Boeing. I've been involved with the space program from its infancy when the U.S. jumped into the Space Race in 1958 and Rocketdyne's propulsion systems powered the rocket that launched the first American satellite into space. My job was to hire rocket scientists and engineers who would develop propulsion systems capable of landing man on the moon. Today, these engines, the F1 and J2, are on display at the Smithsonian.

I've witnessed shuttle launches from test stands at Kennedy Space Center and watched engineers operate the mind-boggling, hi-tech instrumentation panels in Mission Control in Houston. I also supported the effort to build the first shuttle engines and later watched the mighty power of those engines lift the shuttle into space. I've cried tears of joy at our successes, and wept at the tragedy and deaths of our NASA co-workers. I've met and talked with several of our astronauts and held moon rocks in my hands.

After 35 years, I retired from Boeing in 1994, only to return a year later as a full-time consultant in their Human Resources Department, where I remain today, but hopefully not for too much longer—I am counting the days. It was a memorable experience having been a part of a team that worked with the space pioneers who had a vision and made it happen. But, as the saying goes, "It's time to stop and smell the roses."

I live in Calabasas, CA, which is only a short drive through a mountain pass to the ocean—a great haven when in need for "space" or "quiet time." I enjoy strolling the beaches, watching the breakers and occasionally spotting a migrating whale. It is here I think about and plan for the future. I am overwhelmed by my list of "things to do." Though our skin and bones will change with the years, I shall always try to remain "forever young." There is still much to do and see, even in retirement. It is a happy time when the ANVIL arrives. Reading through it brings back many wonderful memories.

How Your Class Year Makes You Unique

Ed Styles • Class of 1944 • Alexandria, VA

I read your class breakdown of ANVIL circulation. World War II might have been expected to cast such a blight over WHS in the early 1940's that none of us would want to revisit those years. but it seems to have had the opposite effect. Why are we disproportionately interested in that period, I wonder.

Perhaps because (1) during our Depression-era childhood, unending privation seemed our inevitable destiny; (2) with our adolescence came the wartime boom, which elevated our dreams along with the economy; (3) we were perhaps the first generation to have had from birth nearly continuous access to radio and movies, which despite their meretriciousness did give us glimpses into possibilities beyond those afforded by the Harbor; and (4) horrible as it was, the war itself progressed from initial defeat toward ultimate triumph, perhaps unifying us and liberating us from some of the lunacy natural to teenagers.

In other words, I wonder if the shift from hopelessness to hope gave us a lift unknown to those who have experienced only the comparative affluence of the post war world.

As a historian, what do you think?

Adventures In Internship

Harold Goodman • Class of 1942 • Los Angeles, CA

Did I tell you that I once examined Marilyn Monroe? You gotta be at the right place at the right time.

I was an intern at the old Cedars of Lebanon Hospital. That month I was on what was called the private surgical service. One of the duties of this service was to do the official hospital history and physical on new patients. Of course, the admitting doctor had already done his own, but, this was a teaching hospital.

Who should come in with acute appendicitis? You guessed it. I buttoned up the neck of my white jacket that was usually left unbuttoned, knocked on the room door and found three men at bedside. They were politely asked to leave and I was alone with her. Hair up in curlers, vanishing cream on her face, no make-up. She had a bellyache but was very cooperative. I asked every question I could think of then felt her tummy. "Does this hurt? I'm going to let go now and tell me if that hurts more." Very professional.

Like a damned fool, I didn't make a xerox of the sheets. They would have been proof. Believe me, it really happened.

Rabwin and Rosenbloom were the team. They were among the best surgeons in L.A. Rosenbloom loved to torture interns who were "third assistants" at surgery. He quizzed as the two of them cut and snipped. I was holding retractors and he asked, "What is the alkaline tide?" I couldn't remember. Hell, I didn't want to become a surgeon anyway. I can't stand the sight of blood. Bobby can't either. He was visiting L.A. and I took him in to watch a Cesarian—gowned and masked. After a while, I glanced over. He was pale. I led him out to the corridor, sat him on the floor with his head between his knees. He'll deny it, but it is true.

House staff has it easy these days. First, they get a living wage. We were kept barefoot and broke and fed scraps from the kitchen. There was no such thing as disposables. Interns were set to work reaming out and sharpening used hypodermic needles. Used glass syringes had to be washed and resterilized. We did our own blood counts on battered microscopes. Now they have fancy machines that do it. One-hundred-hour work weeks were as nothing. Sleep? Forget it. We were married right after the internship. I could hardly stand in front of the rabbi. I've never fully recovered.

Jo Idzkowski • Class of 1945 • Jackson, MI

Family obligations prevented my wife and I from attending both the summer picnic and the reunion of the class of 1945. From all reports I have read, both were well attended and enjoyed by all. Each issue of the ANVIL stirs up memories, mostly good, of places, events and people. Keep up the good work. When Jimmy Platis runs out of things to do, maybe he could do a little research on some of the neighborhood recreational softball teams that were so common in the late 1930s and early 1940s. Teams such as the Red Wings, Ivy Indians Nebulaes, American Slovak Civic Club, The Canteen Club and others. There were also several outstanding teams and players in the recreational basketball leagues in the Calumet Region, in the days when people participated in amateur sports for fun rather than watching overpaid pros on TV.

Ice House Club
The Ice House Club was located at 140th and Main Street. (L to R): Louise Misik, Arthur "Red" Lukaszewski, John "Stooge" Suda, Vince "S. M." Kerrin, Stan "Pita" Czapcyk, Joe "Chic" Furto, (Kneeling) Ted Nowesnick.

192

Cheerleading in 1943 & 1946

Sylvia (Kuzman) Kuta • Class of 1946 • Bourbonnais, IL

Students looked forward to the end of each school week (today's T.G.I.F.) because Friday evenings meant going to the football or basketball games with friends or dates.

During the 1943 season, the WHS football team had an unbeaten season (9 wins, 0 losses) and were State Champs, beating South Bend Washington 27-6. Leading the excitement were cheerleaders George Marchuk, Helen Monea, Lorraine Kirilova and Millie Zientara.

In 1944, the new varsity cheerleading squad consisted of Lorraine Kirilova, Maggie Michaels, June Shep and Sylvia Kuzman; they were acclaimed as the best in the Calumet Region by adding dance steps to the traditional squats and leaps.

In 1945, June Shep and Sylvia Kuzrnan had new teammates: Goldie Mate, Sylvia Simon, Ann Belmonte and Paul Guiden, who helped refine the new cheerleading art. Novel cheerleading development continued in 1946 and was noted by Frank Reynolds, then a sports broadcaster on Radio Station WJOB, and sports writers in South Bend, Lafayette, Indianapolis, and people all over the district. Four of the girls received cheerleading scholarships to Indiana State Teachers College (now Indiana State University) in Terre Haute. Sylvia Kuzman also received a four-year cheerleading scholarship from Northwestern University for her aerial and jump-rope acrobatic routines. It was the first time Northwestern ever offered such a scholarship and its football teams went to the Rose Bowl the next two years.

Memories of the "Rag Man"

Margaret M. Christenson • Class of 1942 • Griffith, IN

I just couldn't let the March issue of the ANVIL go by without responding to the cartoon of the "Rag Man." I never was quite sure what he was calling—I thought it was something about an "old lion." Living near Washington Park and hearing the "old lion" roar once in a while bolstered this theory. And seeing his burlap bags with lumpy knobs sticking out all over, I was sure he had chunks of naughty children in the bag. If I was out in the back yard when he came down the alley, I would make a dash for the lilac bushes to hide under them. That wasn't very smart as they were just inside the fence from the alley. Glad all this was straightened out after all these years!

194

Talk About Coincidences

Mike Macesich • Class of 1946 • Normal, IL

I had graduated in June of 1946 and promptly enlisted in the Marines. I met several WHS alums at the swearing in, including Mitch Stolarz, Ernie Floor, Andy Hrick, and Eddie Mihalko. We spent boot camp together and in February of 1947, we were sent to San Francisco for assignment overseas. We had two days liberty and Mitch and I decided to hit the bars in Frisco one afternoon. After hitting a few places we decided to have one more and stopped again. We are enjoying ourselves when up walks this gorgeous woman who says, "Aren't you Mike and Mitch from WHS?" We were stunned! We found out very quickly that we were talking to Miss McFeely, one of WHS's most ogled, eyed, leered and dreamed-about office clerks.

Another Coincidence

Michael Arsulich • Class of 1946 • San Diego, CA

Frank: Your March issue of recognizing your brother's gait reminded me of a similar incident that happened to me in early September, 1952, in Taequ, Korea. I was in the transient area waiting for assignment to our next unit. There were about 50 of us. I noticed our sergeant walking around waiting like the rest of us. His facial features resembled a family I knew on the 49th block of Alexander Avenue. I let it

195

pass.

A few days later, four of us were eating at our table for dinner. After talking awhile, this sargent asked me, "Where are you from?"

I replied, "East Chicago, Indiana."

"Hot Dog!" he said.

I looked at him and said, "You're Arpad Szaller, aren't you?"

He answered, "Yes, I am!"

After much discussion, not having seen him for 10 years, I asked, "Why did you ask where I was from?"
He said that he had seen me walk. He had seen my gait in his past but couldn't recall where. Later, back at home, I asked some buddies about my distinctive walk.

He said, "Yes, you do have a distinctive walk. You walk like you've got it made!"

After 50 years, I do "have it made."

Hey! Let's Think About It

Jack Culver • Class of 1946 • Griffith, IN

Think about what?
- Remember your first prom?
- Remember when you bought your first pair of shoes with stamps (Father and Son) during the war?
- Remember your first kiss? With WHO?
- Your favorite song and why?
- What happened at Larry's/Sardi's at 139th and Main Street?
- Wells Street Beach—Mike Maluga, Harry Snedden and I (Gully) cleaned the beach on the weekends for Gus. He gave us breakfast for that task.
- Who rode in the American Legion 1928 Packard touring sedan owned by Steve "Stosh" Cvitkovich and Harry Snedden? We had to measure the gas in the tank with a yardstick. We

196

charged 25 cents a ride to help fill the tank.

- Who did you walk home with after school? Did you hold hands and get a smooch?

Did we have fun or did we have fun? Come on, send in your thoughts to the P.O. Box number in Griffith. [WHS Alumni Assn., P.O. Box 505, Griffith, IN 46319]

What about our teachers? Some were strict, some were easy.

Sam Geddes came to one of our class reunions. I asked him, "Sam, did you ever find out who cut the top section of your car steering wheel out?"

He said, "Jack!! Was that you?'

"No, Mr. Geddes."

Bob Heine and Elmer Lucas were pushing my mom's Twin City Floral Truck down Main Street. We wanted to get it started. Then we found out it was out of GAS. Those two friends just about killed me. What did you do in the hallways? Cordovers Tucker and I would bump foreheads when we would meet. What did you do? Who was your worst/best teacher? You see we from "Da Harbor" could go on and on with no end about the good/bad times we had. Come on and tell us about "Your Good Ole Times." We all want to hear from you.

If you really want to hear some good ones come on down to the "Romeo's." We meet on the odd numbered months (Jan., March, May, July, etc.) on the second Tuesday of that month at noon at Aurelios on N. Calumet Avenue in Hammond. Call me at 219-922-7303 or Larry Field 219-763-6912. Keep smiling! It's easier.

Nature's Triumph

Bob Krajewski • Class of 1946 • Munster, IN

"A sixteen-year-old girl is a smash triumph of nature." I don't remember when or where I first encountered this incredibly perceptive observation. My literary perusal for the source was a loss. Perhaps it came from our oldest philosophers—Plato or Aristotle; perhaps it came from one of our currently well regarded philosophers—Jay Leno or Walter Dee. In any event, based on recollections of my four years at WHS, that statement is as true as the law of gravity or the proof of the speed of light. My own perceptions of this everlasting truth were sharpened even before WHS; they began at Riley School. A very pretty WASP speech teacher, Miss Daniels, commented that she was struck by how beautiful the girls were at Riley. She ventured that one of the reasons for this might be due to the unusual ethnic mix of the students; she had never been in a similar situation. I believe that was the day my hormones really kicked in.

At our 40th reunion I was chatting with a classmate, and we were reminiscing about former friends with the usual questions about who married who and what jobs they have and the fun we had. And then she said, "And weren't we all so beautiful?" I could only nod dumbly in agreement, unable to put into words my reaction which was so in tune with hers. I honestly cannot recall who I spoke with, but I do recall she was one of those sixteen-year-old beauties!

One could be a rater of the prettiest girls merely by being a perceptive observer in one's regular classrooms. However, that would severely limit the pool of potential subjects. In any scientitic analysis, the larger the sample of subjects tested, viewed or evaluated, the more confident one can be of the results; otherwise one gets involved in some very tricky small sample statistical treatments. But I digress.

198

Realizing that I had to expand my horizons, I had to plan carefully; I had to schedule classes where the girls were. Electives had to be wisely chosen; that truth became clear after one wasted, illogical semester in electric shop. Extra curricular activities were another option. Since I had no instrumental or vocal music talents, I scheduled art classes and became a staffer on both the WEEKLY and the SENIOR ANVILs. My efforts we rewarded!

There probably are quite a few girls who wondered why their personal interview never showed up in the WEEKLY ANVIL. Many were persuaded to pose for potential picture spreads in the SENIOR ANVIL. Frequently my camera had no film; after all, it was wartime and film was often scarce. I don't believe I fooled most of them.

Also, I worked hard to gain a good citizenship rating so I could get a hall monitor's post. What an observation point! I could challenge and chat up any lovely who passed by. Having gained then a good reputation for devotion to duty, I finally got a hall monitor's posting as a main office runner. The entire school was then my experimental field. I was able to roam everywhere and enter classrooms of under- and upperclassmen (women) who would not typically be in my purview. Assignments to deliver messages to shop classes were delegated to-subordinates. Occasionally I was reprimanded for taking too long on simple errands, but I was always sufficiently obsequious to avoid losing my post.

My next installment of the report of my scientific analysis will treat at least two other venues of observational techniques—Wells Street Beach and the substitute's bench of athletic teams.

Sweet Sixteen

Bob Krajewski • Class of 1946 • Munster, IN

To recap briefly, last month I gave my personal reactions to a powerful maxim that has reverberated throughout the ages: "A sixteen-year-old girl is a smash triumph of nature."

Further, I demonstrated the use of two venues I used at WHS to observe those beauties: Becoming a staff member of both the WEEKLY and SENIOR ANVILs, and joining the hall and office monitor groups.

There were two other areas I used to perfect my observational skills: Wells Street Beach and the substitutes bench at football and basketball games. All right, Wells Street was certainly not part of the WHS campus, but I spent so much time there that it seemed to be. I spent an incredible number of carefree hours there, and somehow believed that only a favored and select few from the WHS classes of the mid 1950s knew or cared about it. I found out not too long ago that it was a goal of classes in the 1930s.

One didn't need to be secretive about girl-watching at the beach, but it surely brought giggles and a turn-off if a guy was caught staring, gaping and drooling. Therefore, I quickly learned what every beach bum in the world uses to observe, ogle and rate sixteen-year-old beauties—sunglasses and a baseball cap. One only need set a blanket not too far from the water's edge, recline gracefully and watch the lovelies walk by in either direction, all the while pretending to observe the tide coming in.

A camera was always good as a conversational icebreaker, but there always seemed to be a guy around the prettiest girls with a real camera and real film to spoil my approach.

One other area needs analysis—the substitute's bench at athletic contests. I suffered through freshman football and basketball substitute benches, knowing there were usually very few fans (girls) in attendance, because I was looking forward to the following years. And there were more fans (and cheerleaders, too) at those junior varsity football games. And I dressed for a varsity game or two, also. However, it finally dawned on me, in a cosmic rush, that I couldn't enjoy the cheerleaders because they performed BEHIND the substitute's bench, on the track between the bench and the fans!

That discovery, coupled with a lack of talent and desire, led me to drop football as an ogling venue and concentrate on basketball, a true Indiana sport that is performed indoors, where it's warm and the girls don't wear bulky coats and babushkas. Here I enjoyed three seasons with a perfect seat next to all the action. And what years they were! The first year, Vince Boryla stormed on the scene, and the crowds were tremendous. And I enjoyed the games too. I was able to perfect my observational skills, because I knew I would only get in a game when we were hopelessly ahead or completely out of it. That seldom happened, and I believe I held the record on the team for the fewest minutes, make that seconds, played during the season. The next two years I played a little more, usually when Ray Ragelis got in foul trouble or he got a cramp, but that didn't interfere with my then mastery of observation. I even began to wear glasses, "All the better to see you with, my dear." We had a glorious season.

Sometimes the games were so intense I hardly noticed our or the other team's cheerleaders. Our away games were usually packed and one could not avoid noticing that other schools, too, had their share of sixteen-year-old girls, but Coaches Irwin and Baratto always had pre-game talks and the bus left immediately after the game.

The editors requested I name a few at the top of my rating sheets, but I declined lest I forget an important name or two; besides, you all know who you are.

Healthy In Arizona

Lloyd "Lou" Holtzman • Class of 1940 • Scottsdale, AZ

I'm sorry that I couldn't come to the picnic this year. However, enclosed is my yearly contribution for the Monthly ANVIL that is so great to receive and remind us of roots in "Da Harbor." Which also reminds me about the time that I wanted to join the Navy in 1945. I had just heard that my best friend, Frank Onco, class of 1940, was shot down and I was just devastated. We had been close buddies through scouting, grade school and high school, and roommates at Purdue.

I had been involved as a research engineer for the Navy at Douglas Aircraft Company in El Segundo, CA, on a special project to eliminate "Flutter in the Aircraft," which was very important at that time, but I was a civilian and when we lost Frank, I was so upset that I wanted to get in uniform and go in action! The only trouble was that I was in poor health. My blood pressure was 66/44 and my vision was 4/20, which means that I could only see at four feet what I should see at 20 feet.

From one of my friends, I found a doctor that specializes in improving your vision by doing different exercises and I had to do these in his office for 40 hours a week. I had some vacation time owed to me, so I used it to get my eyesight in shape. One of the exercises was to close both eyes and rest my cheekbones on the palms of my hands. (This was called Palming). Think of a pendulum moving slowly back and forth. Well, instead I thought of my girlfriend in a white dress on a swing moving back and forth, and guess where the swing was? It was at the Lakefront Park in "Da Harbor" as I remembered it as a kid. I did this exercise most of my life. When I became married, I would imagine my wife, Rita, doing it at the Lakefront Park in "Da Harbor." In due time, my vision became 20/20 for most of my life and I never needed glasses.

If your eyes get tired from reading or watching TV or whatever, this exercise will rejuvenate your eyes, but it takes deep concentration and your eyes will soon move with the swing. Through the years, I found out that there are so many things that one can do to improve your health. Of course it's best to start early in life. I have been lucky. At nearly 80 years of age, I play tennis two hours a day, three days a week in Scottsdale throughout the year, even when the temperature hits 110 degrees; and they say that I still run like teenager.

So, please take my word, if you are overweight, do something about it. If you are diabetic or have high or low blood pressure, do whatever you can to IMPROVE YOUR HEALTH BEFORE IT'S TOO LATE. Take care!

Depression Anecdotes

Bob Krajewski • Class of 1946 • Munster, IN

Most of our alumni group were touched by the economic depression of the 1930s. Some graduated from WHS just in time to face those hard times; some passed through their school years in the heart of it; some, like me, were in elementary school for most of it. Our youngest members probably heard a fund

Harbor Memories: The Itinerant Knife Sharpener

of stories about those times.

Those personal and family anecdotes usually center about the themes of scrambling to find a job, making do with what you had, squeezing nickels and dimes, eking out a living, and just surviving. Being a certified tightwad in those days was a badge of honor! Not too long ago, the *National Enquirer* ran a contest to identify the champion cheapskate in the USA. There were many clever entries, but the winner was a true champ. He bought a brand of toilet tissue proudly advertised as a double roll; he carefully unrolled those double rolls and re-rolled them into single tissue rolls. I don't know if he was originally from the Harbor.

One of my favorite anecdotes of making do within an educational framework came from a colleague who was a principal in a small Indiana town. During the depression, his superintendent would pick wild berries to make ink for the school's offices.

Years ago, one of the custodians at Franklin School related how he was able to save a few bucks annually on his utility bill. He lived in an upstairs apartment located near a street light. He could read his newspaper by its light without having to switch on the lights in his home.

The word evidently went out to all teachers in the East Chicago Schools to economize whenever possible. It was easy to get their cooperation, because they were frequently paid in scrip, a form of promissory note, which retailers might redeem only with a discount. I can recall teachers keeping watch over the toweling dispenser to make certain that each pupil would use only one paper towel after the bathroom break.

Those economies were practiced by the entire staff at Riley School, I'm sure. Remember how the pencils we got from our book rental fees were distributed? In every class where pencils were used, they were gathered up at the end of class, bundled up by rows, and stored away for the next day.

204

You got the same pencil the next day because a sliver about an inch long was cut at the pencil's end for your name.

In Dr. Mintz' class (then Mr. Mintz) you had to get his permission before you could sharpen your pencil. If he believed you could get another hour or two out of that stub, he denied access to the sharpener. The schools couldn't afford to have us depleting the book rental fund just because we wanted a sharp pencil point. Probably a wise move, because a defective sharpener could grind away a half a pencil before you realized it. As I recall, most of the sharpeners didn't work anyway. Do kids still use pencils?

All to the point—almost all of us have a personal or family anecdote about surviving the Great Depression, and we would all like to hear them. For example, I enjoyed Jack Culver's report that they would move whenever his mother found an apartment with a rent 50 cents cheaper than their current one.

Ted Nowesnick—Better than the Majors!

Mike Arsulich • Class of 1946 • San Diego, CA

I missed the 55th class reunion that was held last month. I noticed the passing of Ted Nowesnick, class of 1946.

I knew Ted when we had several classes together. Let me preface this letter before I get any further. Those of us who played Kiwanis and American Legion baseball in the summer of 1943 were invited to see some of our locals host the visiting Great Lakes Naval baseball team. Their players were all major league players that were inducted into the Navy for the duration of the war. This team included the great Johnny Mize, first baseman for the St. Louis Cardinals.

Our pitcher, Mike Bajo, later told me that when Mize swung at the ball, he could actually hear the "swish" of the bat. No other batter ever impressed him like Johnny Mize.

The game was held at Block Stadium where a fence was recently built in right field some 300 feet to separate play from the General American Tank Car Corporation (GATX).

Each time when Mize came up to bat, he would stare at that fence. We all knew what he had in mind. That hit never came to pass as our Mike Bajo held him at bay.

Within a couple of years, at a high school game, Ted Nowesnick hit a home run in right field that cleared the fence. He told us that he knew it was hit well after he connected. He accomplished a feat that a great major leaguer could not!

The Great Car

Gerald Wenzel • Class of 1947 • Chesterton, IN

Anyone who hung around the Lax family (Sunnyside) during the decade of the forties would sooner or later come into contact with their car. It was about a 1938 Hudson Terraplane. It will be referred to hereafter as the "great car."

My first meeting with the "great one" was December 7, 1941, and everyone knows what happened on that day. Mrs. Lax came in to pick us up at the Indiana Theater along with Jack and David Lax to give us a ride home to Sunnyside. She mentioned that Ronald Lax had heard over the radio that the Japanese had bombed Pearl Harbor. Remember, the world was much larger in those days, but we had been expecting to become involved with the war in Europe, not with the Japanese in SE Asia. Little did we know that this would affect all of our lives for the next fifty years. But it didn't take long to sink in.

The "great car" was to become a major factor in all of our lives during WWII. First, I must explain a few things. This automobile was just not your usual car. It was part humanoid, part extraterrestrial and part animal—as in a mule, stubborn as or strong as. It certainly could not be taken for granted, if so it would balk. So, a baseball bat was always kept on the floor of

206

the car, called the "persuader." That way if the starter didn't work—and usually it didn't—drastic steps would have to be taken. The driver would get out of the car with the persuader in hand and give a good whack in the area of the gas tank. The word was "not too high, not too low, not too hard, not too slow." It had to hit in a specific spot and only a member of the Lax family could perform this operation (meaning Jack, David, Ronald and later Bruce). Then he would go around to the front end and give the radiator a good whack the same way. And it worked! So we were off to our destination. Now we have all seen the joke where about ten midgets all pile out of the car. Well, how about a dozen high school boys?

Seeing as this was wartime with gas rationing, etc., we went mostly around Lake County and usually to basketball games. WHS had excellent teams at the time, so those were normally happy days. Also we had blackouts or air raid drills (remember these?) As it so happened, one of our friend's fathers was an air raid warden, which entitled him to have a five-gallon fire extinguisher. Naturally this piece of equipment came in handy for our needs. We would fill it up with water and then drive around corners squirting everyone in sight. This device would shoot out about twenty-five feet!

Then there was the time when Jack Lax was driving going west on Chicago Avenue and somehow we ended up on the sidewalk near the downtown East Chicago area. Remember this was "enemy" territory and the people in East Chicago didn't appreciate our Indiana Harbor sense of humor. How many times have you ever seen these people from East Chicago (other than to go to work) in the Harbor? Never, as I recall.

In August about 1949 I was attending St. Joseph College (Rensselaer, IN) and we were going through football practice. It's always hot and dusty in August and nobody ever came to see us practice. But, low and behold, here comes the "great one" in a cloud of dust right onto the practice field—

almost running over three players. Nobody could believe this was happening. Dick Scharf was the consummate gentleman. He never got flustered about anything. The very gregarious Marty Sherman jumped out of the car, ran over and introduced himself to Coach Scharf. Being a practical man, the coach decided it was time for a break anyway. The driver of the car, David Lax, seemed to mutter something like "damn, I got to fix those brakes one of these days."

Now I could go on for hours telling stories about the "great car," and I'm sure others could add stories of their own. So don't hesitate to let us know about them.

Harold "Flash" Taylor, class of 1947, related a story about how he and his father were walking home from church (138th and Hemlock) on a Sunday morning. They were walking south on Grand Boulevard near WHS. Here comes the "great car" containing the entire Lax family and some neighbor kids. They too were coming home from church on north Grand Boulevard. The Taylors were invited to "hop in" as both the Laxes and Taylors were headed home to Sunnyside. Mr. Taylor was somewhat taken aback by the number of people in the car (now about ten) but it didn't bother Harold or anybody else. By this time, they were used to it.

1946—A Watershed Year for Just About Everyone

Gerald Wenzel • Class of 1947 • Chesterton, IN

The entire world was in a chaotic state after World War II ended in August 1945. It would never return to what it had been before the war. Returning servicemen wanted to get some of the "dolce vita," and this would not come about for a few more years.

We had been on a wartime economy for four years, as the war demanded the development of ships, tanks, planes, guns and ammunition. America's first priority was to win the war. Everyone knew there would be shortages of just about everything that was not war-related. By this time, many of us were becoming impatient. Those of us who were on the home front didn't have it so bad, but those who were in Tom Brokaw's "Great Generation" had things much tougher. During the thirties, it was the Depression and then along came the war in the forties. So, there had been about 15 years of "making do" and they were growing tired of this.

Many of our ANVIL subscribers are in this great generation. So, it took about four to five years before anyone could buy a new car, house or household appliances. In the meantime, there was this new thing just coming out, "television," and of course, many young couples were getting married since the uncertainties of the war were behind them. For those of us who were still in high school, it was time to start some football physical conditioning because it was now early August and regular practice would start August 15th. Classes would start the day after Labor Day. Traditionally, the-future football players would meet after work in the mills, at Washington Park. Anyone else who wanted to come was welcome. 1946 was not your normal year, so we had several G.I.'s out there too. None of these workouts would be supervised by any coaches. We were on our own as far as the conditioning went. It usually consisted of a little jogging, some pushups, the usual stuff.

Then, we'd end it with a touch football game. After that, we'd sit around for a while and the '"old-timers" would tell a few stories about how it was in the "old days." There was great camaraderie and everyone enjoyed these sessions. We usually had about ten to twenty guys out there. For some reason I brought my camera and took pictures that day. These are the ones who were there: Alex Akim, Ben Brown, Mehilo Keseley, Milan Chobanov, Joe Zeman, Bob Masulovich, Tom Delor, Jim Miannovich, and Mike Dotlich with his son,

"Shorty."

This was about 56 years ago. If any family member would want these pictures, contact me. My name is in the directory.

Senators vs. Jasper

Mike Macesich • Class of 1946 • Normal, IL

It was a cold, snowy, late January day in 1946 and the Senators were to play a game against Jasper at Jasper, Indiana. We left East Chicago early that Thursday morning. We were to play a Thursday game and then again Friday at Jeffersonville. The snow got progressively worse as the day grew longer. Somehow our bus driver got us lost and spent several hours on twisting, narrow, hilly roads looking for Jasper. It was more than once that the driver had to stop and back up to be able to make a curve in the road. We finally got there at 9:00 pm to be met by a full house of disgruntled fans. The agreement: We spent the night in Louisville and had a State Police escort to Jasper the next day. We were again greeted by a raucous full house of Jasper fans. We won both games that night and went on to win both at Jeffersonville the next night.

Great Depression Memories

Harold F. Goodman, M.D. • Class of 1942 • Angeles, CA

When I was about ten ears old (1935), Mom sent me to the grocery store with a 50-cent piece. It was meant to supply the makings for dinner. There were five of us. Naturally, she chose me to do the shopping, I being more responsible than my brothers. Naturally, I took shortcuts through alleys. The half-dollar fell through a hole in my pocket and I spent the remainder of the daylight hours searching for it. Talk about being devastated.

210

When times got better, each of us was given a dime for the Indiana Theater's Saturday matinee. Later we got a nickel to supplement our enjoyment of the twice-watched double feature, the comedy, the cartoon, the serial, the coming attractions and Harry Tarler live on stage to give away prizes and sing along with the bouncing ball on the screen. We stomped and whistled when the projectionist fell asleep. One Saturday, I swallowed my nickel. Never found it, though I tried.

From Stanford, California

Gerald Reaven, M.D., Professor of Medicine • Stanford University

Although I never graduated from WHS, I was in the class of 1946. However, I grew up in the Harbor, went to elementary, junior high and high school through the 10th grade at WHS, and both my brother and mother (class of 1920!) graduated from WHS. As you can see, I have many ties to both the school and the community.

I did get a chance to talk with Vinnie Boryla, and I thank you (Frank Hanak) for your help in connecting us. There were a group of kids who grew up and played ball together around 141st and Euclid. I was among that group, which contained Davey (Yosh) Brennan and Ed Martell, as well as Vinnie; all three contributed to the WHS basketball program. I had not seen or talked to Vinnie since his son ended his football career at Stanford. We had a good telephone conversation. I think what you and Archie started is great.

Reactions To Articles In The ANVIL

Lee Edelman Fink • Class of 1947 • Van Nuys, CA

Frank: Needless to say, you have done a terrific job. I don't think you realize the impact these ANVIL letters have on us.

It stimulates such memories as:
1. Oh yes, I remember that guy.
2. I wonder who she married? She was so pretty.
3. What a teacher! Dignified, yet not stodgy.
4. What a scholar—he (or she) should have gone a long way.
5. I heard the war took him. He's a hero in my mind, and probably in many others and Mother's.
6. Such a good principal, and his assistant, such a good V.P.
So, Frank and staff, thanks for the memories!

Jumping Ship in the WHS Pool

Lee Edelman Fink • Class of 1947 • Van Nuys, CA

It would be difficult for me to express the amount of enjoyment that I derive from reading each issue. What a joy it is to read about classmates and others in places far and near. I cannot send this to you without a memory of WHS.

My attendance at WHS was from 1943-47. Apparently, the Phys. Ed. Department thought that all of us girls were going to jump from burning ships, because in order to pass Miss Wolf's swim class, we all had to jump from the balcony into the deep end of the pool. My memory is of a group of us standing there in mortal terror until it was our turn.

Twice a week I attend a water exercise class and as I step into the warm and comforting water, I think about that leap! It is somewhat like a bad dream; however, we all survived and went on to other challenges.

Thank you staff, for all the pleasure that you provide for so many of us.

Incidentally, my husband and I are both docents at the Autry Museum of Western Heritage and should any alumni come this way, please feel free to contact us. We are in the phone book (818-781-3465).

Fashion Sense

Bob Krajewski • Class of 1946 • Munster, IN

I believe I was the very first adult to wear walking shorts in East Chicago, excepting only those scout leaders. That was almost 45 years ago, but I remember the day very clearly. It was a day or two after Father's Day in 1956, and Marge, keeping up with the latest men's fashions in magazines published in the East, had given me a beautiful pair of chicken pants! Yes, chicken pants. Did you ever hear of them? It's an old term, not too common, but my oldest brother used to bug me whenever I, as a seven- or eight-year-old, wore short pants or as he labeled them, "chicken pants." Derivatively, the term probably grew out of the perception that too many guy's legs looked as scrawny as chicken legs when they wore them.

As I recall, when I grew up in the Harbor, from the age of about ten until voting age (then 21), the only people I saw in chicken pants were very young children, Boy Scouts on duty and a very few of their adult leaders. I would have preferred going three rounds with Frank Loar rather than subject myself to the humiliating and public scorn and finger-pointing if seen in public wearing them.

All of those long buried thoughts about chicken pants surfaced, but I was newly married and about the serious business of pleasing Marge. It was not without some trepidation that I set out with our ten-month-old daughter, Susan, and her stroller for a walk to downtown E.C., where we were then living. I had just crossed Magoun Avenue at Chicago in front of what was then Ben Lipman's Men's Store when I noticed two teenage girls approaching me. When they saw me, they stopped, gasped, wiped tears of laughter from their eyes, pounded each other on the back, and almost fell through Ben's plate-glass window. Susan gurgled with delight; something funny was happening!

I summoned reserves of poise and proceeded as if I hadn't noticed their outburst. Glancing back I saw they were now almost erect with their hands on their knees still laughing and pointing. With honesty as a guidepost, I must admit I was quite an apparition to those young ladies. It was probably the first time they had ever seen an adult male in chicken pants; and there he was, this bespectacled 6'3" guy with skinny legs and bony knees, pushing a stroller in chicken pants. A good thing it was broad daylight!

Times change and so do attitudes, because it is quite remarkable to see how many school kids—elementary through high school—break out the shorts on the first day after the holidays when the temperature nears the 50-degree mark. But times do change. We were visiting Susan, getting ready for a round of golf. Since it was a great day with the temperature in the 70's, I put on a pair of shorts. Susan told of the latest fashion trends there, "Dad, only the tourists wear shorts here at this time of year."

Josephine (Grdinich) Mosca • Class of 1941• Highland, IN

I really enjoy getting the ANVIL and reminiscing about "growing up" in the Harbor, summer nights joining the parade down Guthrie Street and Michigan Avenue to the lake front to cool off, and on the way back stopping for a triple-dip cone at Larry's. We walked everywhere—the bus was only for trips to downtown Hammond on Saturdays.

The ANVIL is great and I appreciate all the work it entails by you. I was on the literary staff for our SENIOR ANVIL, class of 1941. Thank you for your hard work.
I'm sorry I wasn't able to go to the Sports Banquet—I would have loved to see and meet with Miss Skrentny. I was in her advanced grammar class diagramming sentences, etc.

214

Wasn't easy—rules of grammar helped me in my work as a secretary later. I can't remember all the rules she drilled to us now but she was good—and firm!

The Wartime Music of the Jerry Russ Orchestra

Barbara Kovack Babas • Class of 1947 • Munster, IN

I was a sophomore in the fall of 1944 and loved to dance. My friend Charlotte Canamar heard about the teenage dances at Garfield School, and so we went to check it out. There I met Ray Bobin, a real smooth dancer. I was flattered when he asked me to dance, and we became friends. And that's how it started for me.

Ray's friend, Johnnie Irk, was a drummer with a dance band of his own, and, they needed a piano player. Ray knew that I played classical piano, having taken lessons for many years, and he took me to the band practice at the Croation Hall in Calumet to sit in with the band. I was out of my league in playing this type of music, but I could read music well, had rhythm, loved the big-band sound, and could keep a beat—all in my favor. They must have been desperate because they kept me on. I needed my parent's permission to try this new venture which involved late hours and plenty of trust. There were other bands in high school at that time, but we were the best, though some may dispute this claim. We all agree that no one could play the Clarinet Polka like Bob Heine. But, this is just the start of the story.

Even though some later changes were made, for the most part the band consisted of two alto saxes, Kenny Boldi & Louie Pavelka; two tenor saxes, Gerry Marshall and Salvadore (Chevo) Nunez; three trumpets, John (Moe) Evion, Frank Mehok, and Joe Rico; drums, Johnny Irk; guitar, Jerry Banina; bass, Ronnie Janowski (from Roosevelt); and me on the piano; plus our lovely vocalist, Virginia Hausman. We were the band

and we believed we were great.

The band played at many local dance halls—Croation Hall, Benito Juarez, Elks—and several of the dances at WHS. All were great fun. Playing those groovy jitterbug tunes and watching the kids dance—and the applause!! After a job we would head for Hot Dog John's for a messy and famous hot dog and a chili snack. We each earned on average $2 a job, except New Year's Eve when our pockets bulged with about $10.

A big event for us was appearing in an assembly program in the auditorium for the whole school. As a feature number, we did a take-off on Liszt's Hungarian Rhapsody II where I played the hard parts and the band would toot a couple notes and take all the bows. It was supposed to be funny!

We inherited and adopted Kenny Boldi's uncle, Russell Hanzi, a real, grown-up musician, who led us in rehearsals and began to teach us the ropes. With his leadership and help from a couple other "adult musicians" who occasionally showed up—Georgie Porumb, clarinet, John Trimmel and Bill Rakos, trombones—we developed a good book, joined the Musician's Union and became better organized. Rehearsals moved to the Boy Scout Hut in Calumet. And finally, the name of the band was changed to the Jerry Russ Orchestra (combining the names of Jerry Banina and Russell Hanzi), as our popularity increased in the area.

In fact, word got around to the Army, and through the efforts of Special Services, Sgt. Mike Mihalic, another local boy, we were asked to play for the Halloween Party at the Blythville Air Force Base in Arkansas in October, 1945. WOW!! It meant missing a day of school, and because there were so many of us we didn't dare try to ditch. So, with a letter from the Special Services in hand, we went to the principal's office to get permission. To our surprise, and delight, it was granted. Georgie Porumb agreed to be chaperone and also front the band, and we all received our parent's permission. We were on our way!

216

My mother and Mr. Janowski drove us to Metropolitan Airport (now Midway) and there we boarded a C-47 which was sent specifically just for us. I'll never forget flying in that plane. You could see outside through the seams in the fuselage. There were metal seats along both sides, no fine accommodations here. It rumbled through the skies; so much noise. No jets—just propellers. There was no need to pressurize the cabin because of our low altitude. We could watch the cars below and view the scenery clearly. The servicemen who accompanied us were very friendly, and I was even allowed to sit in the pilot's seat, wear the earphones, and actually hold onto the wheel!!! I couldn't drive a car at that time, and here I was flying a plane. I suppose the co-pilot had everything in control, but nevertheless, it was an experience not shared by many.

At the airbase, the fellows were taken to regular barracks and Virginia and I were housed at the Nurse's Quarters. We shared a nice two-cot room, and though we were bedded down for the night, the sounds of laughter and activity in the main room coming from nurses and the servicemen who were visiting them drifted through our walls far into the night. What went on in there, we shall never know. Our meals were together in the Officer's Mess and the food was pretty good. Virginia and I had privileged use of the base commander's vehicle and driver who took us on a sightseeing tour around the base. It was like having our own private chauffeur, waiting for us outside at every stop. We took a ribbing from the guys who had to rough it—mostly walking or crowded in the back of an army truck when they needed it. Being female had its privilege.

That evening we set up the bandstands and sound equipment in the base hall and then the Halloween Dance began. Those servicemen really loved our big band music while cozying up with the nurses and their girlfriends in a hot muggy hall. No A/C!! We were thrilled and grateful for the opportunity and at the same time proud of doing our bit for the war effort.

Things changed again when Virginia left the band. We added Dick Oros (from RHS) ro replace me and I became the singer. I'll never quite understand how that all came about, but I was glad to stay involved with those fellows who had become companions.

And, what about Ray Bobin? He asked me to his junior prom and the relationship ended shortly after. The band broke up in 1946. After graduation, Jerry continued his lifetime of music with the Star Serenader's and Kenny moved on to Las Vegas. We went our different ways, but those happy memories are mine, and the melody lingers on.

Blythville Air Force Base Gig—October 1945

Back Row: Johnny Irk, Ronnie Janowski, Frank Mekok, John "Moe" Evion, Jerry Banina, Barbara Babas, Joe Rico, Virginia Hausman, Chuck from Air Force Base in Arkansas. Center: Salvadore "Chevo" Nunez. Bottom: Georgia Poraneb, Kenny Boldi, Louie Pavelka, Gerry Marshall, Mr. Janowski.

1949 Senators

Basketball Trailblazers

Mike Macesich • Class of 1946 • Normal, IL

It was state tournament time in late February, 1946. We had won the conference and were top-rated in the area and among the tops in the state. We had to beat Hammond High in the finals of the sectionals, and broke their lock on the championship. Led by Ray Ragelis, Clarence Walker, Buddy Balog, Wimpy Kolina and myself, we won handily. The next week we beat a good LaPorte team to win the regionals. We were on our way to the semi-finals in Lafayette.

Our team left on a Friday in three cars. There was snow on the ground and some slick spots on the highway. A few miles from Goodland, Indiana, we had a blowout on a two-lane road; remember, no steel belts in those days. I was in the front seat holding on for dear life. Thanks to the skill and strength of John Patrick, our AD, we were able to stay on the road and stop safely. We bought a tire in Goodland and made it to Lafayette later that day. We were favorites to win the first game the next day, but we were upset by a team from Culver, Indiana. We had a great season and I like to think 1945-46 basketball Senators were the trailblazers for all the great tournament teams that came later.

Memories of the Indiana Theater

Walter Dee Dudzinski • Class of 1940 • Munster, IN

In the summer of 1939, prior to my senior year at WHS, I was hired as an usher at the Indiana Theater, based on a recommendation by Frank Tamborski, class of 1938, who was an usher at the time. This was my first "professional" job, and my starting salary was 25 cents an hour. They provided me with a uniform jacket, but I had to use my own flashlight.

For 40 hours of work weekly, I brought home, in a little brown envelope, $10.00 less taxes. After three months, my wages were raised to 30 cents an hour. This started my savings for college.

Jack Albertson was the manager and he treated all of us well. The theater was open daily at 12:30 pm. It was beautifully decorated and had a small balcony which was opened only if the downstairs was filled. One of the ushers jobs was to check the balcony periodically when it was closed to make sure there were no lovers up there! Admission into the theater was 25 cents for adults and 10 cents for children. We made the popcorn which sold for 5 cents and 20 cents. Candy bars were 5 cents.

Most often, there were double features except when a long movie, such as "Mr. Smith Goes to Washington" (Jimmy Stewart) was shown. Wednesday evening was ladies night and each got a free dish to build her set. For a while, we also had Bingo night for ladies and men.

Saturday afternoon was kids day, when in addition to the regular movie, there was an "action serial" usually featuring some well known cowboy (remember Hoot Gibson). Each week, the serial would end with a catastrophe about to happen (Gibson ready to go over a cliff) and the following week he miraculously escapes. It brought the kids back week after week.

Remember, back then there was no TV, no computers, no malls, and not too many cars, everybody—adults and kids— came to the theater.

During my senior year, I got a job at the theater for Don Brislain, also class of 1940. Don and I became good friends and that still exists to the present day.

After graduating in June 1940, I left the Indiana Theater and returned only as a paid customer with many fond memories.

Bill Thanholt • Class of 1944 • Crown Point, IN

Frank: Please find my check for the picnic as well as for my contribution to the ANVIL. I think it must be due.

I believe I have found, if not the oldest, one of the oldest living alumni of WHS. However, when she graduated in 1924, it was called East Chicago High School. She is well and sharp. I have forwarded my latest ANVIL to her. Her name is Emma Porter, maiden name, Gansinger. Her father had a jewelry store on the 3500 block of Main Street, which I don't remember. She lives with her daughter, Margaret Adams, here in Crown Point, Indiana.

Keeping Busy in Appleton, Wisconsin

Dorothy Szepanski Walters • Class of 1947 • Appleton, WI

Hi Frank. I would like to congratulate you and your staff for the fantastic job you are doing. I thoroughly enjoy all of the articles in the newsletter, especially the humorous ones. If I still lived in Indiana, I would gladly volunteer. You go above and beyond—making phone calls as in the Sue Tobias/Bob Haugh situation. Soon you'll be known as Mr. Cupid!

Glad you reminded us to look in our checkbooks to see when we sent in our last donation. Seems I am one of the guilty ones. Enclosed is a donation for last year and this year. You know how busy we seniors can be—traveling, family life, fun, etc. May I make a suggestion that works for the Genealogy Society that I belong to? They simply put the expiration date on the address label. It works for me, because I don't want to miss a copy, and I will make sure it is paid. If you don't, they will stop sending the brochures to you.

I have spent a lot of time researching my family tree, making many trips to the National Archives in Chicago. Also, the Family History Center in Mesa, Arizona, and locally. It is very exciting for me when I find information on my extended family. I am constantly on the internet, since Ellis Island records have been posted on there. One big problem is that many, many names are misspelled. You have to try all variations of the names. 1 also have received documents that were downloaded online from new relatives that I met for the first time on the Message Boards.

My parents were born in Poland when it was under Austrian rule, therefore it has been more difficult. I am dealing with three different languages (Polish, German and Latin) that I have to decipher. I am doing this for my 15 grandchildren, and hope to finish before I must go . . .

My children realize what a nearly full-time job this has been for me, so they have no desire to get involved. For me, it is a labor of love.

I bought a book from Archie McKinlay about the Twin Cities a few years ago at the East Chicago Library on Columbus Drive. It was very interesting and informative. Do you know if he has written any more books on the Harbor lately?

Frank, is the 1947 ANVIL still available? I lost mine in one of the moving processes years ago. I hope to come to the 1945/1946/1947 Reunion, Juliettes Luncheon and picnic this year . . .

Keep up the good work!

Memories

Peter Majeski (Myzejewski) • Class of 1943 •
Mishawaka, IN

I wholeheartedly agree with Lorraine Cohen. The use of the term, "Da Harbor" is degrading as far as the English language is concerned. Margaret Christenson is also on the right track. Living in the past is fine for memories, but the future is for improvement.

You might like to add that back "then" in 1930s, you could go to the Garden Theatre and see three features for a

1947 Basketball—WHS vs. Roosevelt
(L to R): Evelyn Ranich, Naadine Trbovich, Pat Widis, Charlotte Bubala, Joan Karas.

dime. This included each and every time two "A" features and always an outstanding western. You went in at 6:30 p.m. and came out at 11:30 pm, all for a dime. I should know—I ushered there for two years and saw all the great western stars of today and yesterday.

Also, I was born and raised in East Chicago. I went to Roosevelt High for two years before moving to The Harbor and finished my last two years at WHS. Both were valuable experiences, and living in both cities was even more valuable for my later life. Both had their pluses and their minuses. However, WHS seemed to offer me more valuable experiences, such asthe debating club, writing for the WEEKLY ANVIL sports column, and being an attorney. I believe Washington was the first to offer defending attorneys to students who got into trouble. I was also able to be politically involved in being a campaign speaker for students running for office.

I did all this while ushering at the Garden Theater, then the Midway Theater, and finally at the Paramount Theater in Hammond. I always got home at midnight, did my homework, went to bed, woke up for class, went to school, and then caught the bus to Hammond at 4:00 p.m. to be ready to work until midnight. I did this seven days a week. The pay was 30 cents an hour. Sometimes I slept and the bus ended up at Inland Steel. The bus driver was always gracious enough to drive past my house and let me off. Talk about memories.

Varsity Basketball: Top Row (l to R) Ciulei, Gillespie, Kirincic, Mroz, Siegle, Lomberger, Barkal, Bottom row (L to R) Gordon, Ervin, Coach Pack, Eisenberg, Tonkovich, Smoljian

1940-41 Senators

The 1940-41 Senator five tied with Lew Wallace for the Western division crown of the N.I.H.S. Conference. The season before, the best Washington basketball team in many a season lost four games: while this year the highly under-rated Senator five lost only five games. In the regular conference standings, Hammond Tech was the only team to accomplish the feat of defeating the Senators twice. The second game between Washington and Hammond was a hectic battle with nearly 4,000 fans watching the contest. The Tech Tigers barely managed to eke out a 25 to 23 victory.

CHAPTER TEN

10

Memories From the 1950s

In 1955, the mid-point of the decade, Dwight Eisenhower was President and Richard Nixon was Vice President. The minimum wage was 75 cents, and life expectancy was 69.6 years. Russia exploded the H-bomb. Disneyland opened in California. Lego blocks were invented, and Jonas Salk developed a polio vaccine.

The best picture of the year was "Marty," and Ernest Borgnine won the Oscar for his role in it. Anna Magnani won hers for her performance in "The Rose Tatoo." Other great movies of the decade: "All About Eve," "La Dolce Vita," "High Noon," "Invasion of the Body Snatchers," "Jailhouse Rock," "Night of the Hunter," "On The Waterfront," "Rashomon," "Rebel Without a Cause," "The Searchers," "The Seven Samurai," "La Strada," "Sunset Boulevard," "Touch of Evil," "Vertigo," "Winchester '73" and "Written on the Wind."

Some of the popular songs ot the decade: "April in Paris," "Chantilly Lace," "Cold, Cold Heart," "I Love You for Sentimental Reasons," "Get Me to the Church on Time," "Getting to Know You," "The Happy Wanderer," "Luck Be a Lady," "Memories Are Made of This," "No Other Love," "Stranger in Paradise" and "Till There Was You."

Other interesting data from that year:

Average income	**$4,137.00**
Gold, per oz.	**$35.00**
New car	**$1,910.00**
Gallon of milk	**$0.92**

Loaf of bread	**$0.18**
Gallon of gas	**$0.23**
Silver, per oz.	**$0.90**
Dow-Jones avg.	**430.00**

1951—That Wonderful Year

Wally Wolak was Class President, Bill Noonan was Vice President, Velma Turoci was Secretary. Harry Truman was President, Alben Barkley was Vice President, Dean Acheson was Secretary of State.

"The Thirteenth Chair" and "Divine Flora" were presented at WHS. "An American in Paris" won the Academy Award for best movie; "The King and I" was the most popular play on Broadway.

Marian Rubies and Virgil Buzea were voted the most athletic. Willie Mays was voted "Rookie of the Year."

Melvin Reaven and Arthur Avington played on the WHS baseball team. Gilbert Fernandez, Virgil Buzea, Eugene Windbush, Alex Liakopoulos and Bill Noonan were members of the football squad; and George Manous, Wally Wolak, Virgil Buzea and Alex Stamatakis played basketball. Tom Vrahoretis, George Harris and Milan Marich also participated. The Giants won the pennant. Matt and Ed Skopiec played in the band. The Top Ten Records were: "Tennessee Waltz" by Patti Page, "How High The Moon" by Les Paul & Mary Ford, "Too Young" by Nat King Cole, "Be My Love" by Mario Lanza, "Because of You" by Tony Bennet, "On Top of Old Smoky," by The Weavers, "If" by Perry Como, "Sin" by Eddy Howard, "Come On-a My House" by Rosemary Clooney, and "Mockin' Bird Hill" by Patti Page. Dean Hess and Gilbert Fernandez were voted best dressed. The girls wore bobby sox, long skirts, rhinestone jewelry, short shorts, rolled-up jeans and men's shirts. The boys wore pegged tailormades, narrow ties and belts, crew cuts or duck-tailed hairdos.

Mary Beth Johnson and Charlene MacDonald were art editors of the SENIOR ANVIL. Paint by number kits and the abstract art of Jackson Pollock became popular.

Leah Olschko, Patricia McKinney, Helen Palmer, Cornell Kapitan, Donald Leavitt, Sally McCormick and Warren Blumenfeld were on the debating team. Richard Nixon presented his famous rebuttal on TV to charges of improper campaign funding. Student Government officers were Gilbert Fernandez, Alex Stamatakis and Vivian Riley. Y-Teen President was Vera Cutean, Secretary was Theresa Grabski with Margaret Lacko participating.

Principal of WHS was Frank E. Cash, Assistant Principal was Mr. Altenderfer and Superintendent of Schools was Mr. Senour. Helen Slomkowski, Dorothy Shabaz, Esther Garcia, June Kozacik, Mary Ann Tominovich, Helen Perry and Carmen DeLaRosa were Girl Counselors. Miss Depew was Dean of Girls.

Joe Buitron, Patrick Gaidor, Robert Dent, Bias Davilla, Douglas Navarro, Ben Diza, Earl Patterson, Herbert Gonzalez, William Wallace and Herbert Bradford were Washington Brothers. Mr. Kellam was Dean of Boys. Steve Paunovich was a member of the Rifle Club. The Korean Conflict was raging.

THE CLASS OF 1951 GRADUATED. THE ATOMIC AGE BEGAN. IT WAS A WONDERFUL YEAR!

Slovak Roots

Don Kosovac • Class of 1952 • Berkeley, CA

Frank: It seems as though you triggered some memories with a return to your family roots in Slovakia. My own recollections do not stem from bloodlines there, but from the two years my wife and I spent behind the Iron Curtain from 1985-1987 in what was then Czechoslovakia. Trips to Eastern Slovakia from Prague, where we lived while assigned to our embassy, were a minimum of a two-day journey by car. Nevertheless, the time spent in travel was well worth it, especially when the picturesque resort of Strebske Pleso at the foot of the High Tatra Mountains was the destination.

Apart from the beautiful scenery, there is a lot of World War II history associated with Slovakia. It was this historical connection that was the basis for our ambassador's annual fall visits there to lay memorial wreaths in honor of our airmen who were shot down over Slovakia en route to the oil fields in Ploesti, Romania. In some cases, the monuments were simply parts of the aircraft, like the prop, inscribed and meticulously maintained by a Slovak farmer in a clearing in a cornfield. The most significant of these wreath layings, however, took place at the Green Mission cabin, high above the village of Polomka. Navy Lieutenant Green headed an OSS contingent that parachuted into the Banska Bistrice area to support the Slovak National Uprising against the Nazis in 1944. When the uprising failed, the Green mission members took refuge in the cabin, but were eventually captured and executed. The ceremony at the cabin site was always a touching reading by the ambassador of the tragic end to the mission.

These recollections of our time in Slovakia are a far cry from connecting with family, but in truth, as we made the rounds to the various wreath-laying sites, the Slovaks in the surrounding villages greeted us like long lost family. Someone once said that one of every five Slovaks has a relative somewhere in the U.S. You're living proof of that. Nazdravi!

Homeroom with Miss Koncz

Margaret Machuca • Class of 1954

If you remember, Miss Koncz was quite a joker. I used to come late to her homeroom class because I was seeing someone in the hall every morning. For the longest time, Gizella would count me absent. And before homeroom was over, she would spot me at a different seat. She would say "Oh, you're here. I guess I just missed you." What I was doing, was sneaking in through the back door on my hands and knees, then found a seat wherever I could. Then one day I was real late. I crawled on my hands an knees, I turned the door knob, pushed open the door very carefully and DING-GA-LING GA-LING!!! She hung bells on the back door!! And she screamed. "GOTCHA!!!"

I'm the last to know!

Hank Machuca • Class of 1954 • Hammond, IN

Recently, my wife decided to play with her computer and was enlarging old photos. One was a picture of me taken in 1938, in front of my aunt's house, 3313 Block Avenue, in the Harbor. I remember that my

Harbor Memories: The first TV set on the block

father took the picture. I was wearing black, high-top leather shoes, with white socks, short pants, and a white shirt topped with a wooly-looking sweater. I don't think they made polyester in those days. The picture showed old lamp posts, cars built in the 1930s, Block Avenue and three buildings. I was so proud of that picture that I took it with me to work out at the Civic Center in Hammond. I showed the picture to a friend of mine, who went to Roosevelt High School. He is 83 years old. Suddenly he burst out laughing. He ran over to the other side of the locker room where some old friends were changing clothes. And they're all laughing!! One of the other elderly gentlemen walked over to me with the enlarged photo. "This building in the background," he said, "Is it 3311 Block Avenue?"

I said, "Yes, it was next door to my aunt's house."

With that, he burst out laughing so loud he almost lost his teeth. "Damn," he said. "That was the biggest CATHOUSE in Indiana!"

I didn't know. I was three years old. Then I read a book by Archibald McKinley, and by god, there it was, 3311 Block Avenue. A cathouse!! I'm so embarrassed!

Bizzarre Memories From Sunnyside

Bruce Lax • Class of 1952 • Copperopolis, CA

My memories of childhood are varied and sometimes too complex to understand. Sometimes they are so bizarre that I have to question whether they are true or are they just an amalgamation of dreams (day and night), reality, or just something someone told me. To me, however, they are absolute.

I grew up in Sunnyside. Many of my early memories, which occurred before high school, included mostly people and events from and/or about Sunnyside or nearby Sunnyside.

Without getting too detailed, let me just give a few

232

examples. We once tied a kite string to the foot of Roscoe, a crow we had somehow captured. and "flew" him like a kite until Mama mercifully came to his rescue. We caught garter snakes; we went to dumps to do what we called rattin,' we adopted stray dogs and kept them in the neighborhood with bits of food; we burned the bulrushes, we tobogganed down a hill out near the dumps on a discarded car fender; we flipped cars on the icy Sunnyside streets and sometimes the rest of Harbor streets, sometimes with only our Sunday-best shoes on our feet (Sunday shoes for most of us were also our everyday shoes).

My brother Ronald and Jimmy Wenzel jumped off the signboard at Cline and Gary Road (it seemed like that signboard was sixteen stories high); we ice skated in the backyards making our own rinks with garden hoses loaned by cooperating neighbors; we hiked to Twin Bridges, Buffington, B.A.B., the cement plant, the viaduct, and Ellis' Pond, Snake River, Cudahy, the Dumps, Cowboy Town and Franklin School. We swam in our ol' swimmin' hole out behind Franklin, making sure not to get too close to the carcass of a deceased dog; we walked to Washington Park and were given "free" kernels, salt and remnants from the popcorn machine. We made a rope elevator to hoist us in the airway above the chimney tops, and once got Marty Sherman up there and actually shook him off. I would not get on the elevator. It's a wonder we all survived!

My wife, Joan (Kundrat), just looked over my shoulder and said nobody will believe those stories. To me, as I said before, everything I've written here is absolutely true and accurate. That and much more. We all are truly blessed to have grown up in such a wonderland as Indiana Harbor. My email is laxlax@caltel.com. I'd love to hear from you!

Yachting, Anyone?

Eileen Dickes Jones • Class of 1955 • Thunderbolt, GA

Frank: I haven't forgotten your request for a short bio, but I just wanted to wait till after the holidays when I thought I would have more time to write. It hasn't quite worked out that way. Enclosed is a check to help expenses for the ANVIL. I do enjoy it and appreciate all the work you and others do on it.

After I graduated from WHS in 1955, 1 attended Hammond Business College for a year. Then I worked at the Union and/or First National Bank for about 10 years, less a little over a year and a half from June 1961 to February 1963, when I sailed around the world on the brigantine, "Yankee," a 96-foot square rigger you may have read about in the NATIONAL GEOGRAPHIC. While on that trip, I met an Australian named Mick Jones who served as the ship's engineer between New Guinea and Mauritius. Mick later came to the states and we were married in June 1965. He worked at O.F. Jordan Co. until about a year later when we went to Los Angeles to help friends of ours sail the brigantine, "Romance," from L.A. to Miami. They had purchased the ship from the movie studio after she had been rigged and used for the movie "Hawaii."

In Miami, Mick worked for Bertram Yachts and we purchased a three-masted schooner which we sailed back from the Bahamas, renovated, and lived aboard for 13 years. We later sailed up to the Savannah area where Mick worked at Thunderbolt Marine, and we managed a couple of short cruises before he died.

Since I couldn't maintain and sail a large wooden boat, I had to sell her and move ashore. Later, I owned a nice little 30-foot yacht for awhile, and also worked at Thunderbolt Marina.

At present, I still have my house in Thunderbolt, and

have been able to do a little cruising with friends (some Caribbean on the "Romana," plus East Coast, Great Lakes, Pacific NW, Alaska "panhandle," and canals in England) but my main activities are dog-related. I work for a groomer, and have shown my Cardigan Welsh Corgis in breed, obedience and agility. Of course, my dog's main function is pet and companion, the rest is just fun for both of us.

After Dad, coach Herman Dickes, died, my mother moved to Illinois to live with her sister. I used to get up there annually, and we made a few trips back to the Harbor, but now they are both gone. I don't know when I'll get up there again. Maybe I can swing it for some future reunion.

Don't Take Life Too Seriously

Arthur Levan • Class of 1954 • Munster, IN

1. Experience is something you don't get until just after you need it.
2. A day without sunshine is like . . . night.
3. If at first you don't succeed, then skydiving isn't for you.
4. 42.7% of all statistics are made up on the spot.
5. 99% of lawyers give the rest a bad name.
6. I drive way too fast to worry about cholesterol.
7. He who laughs last thinks slowest.
8. I intend to live forever—so far, so good.
9. When everything is coming your way, you're in the wrong lane and going the wrong way.
10. No one is listening until you make a mistake.
11. On the other hand . . . you have different fingers.
12. Love may be blind, but marriage is a real eye-opener.

Late Nights on Euclid Avenue

Art Goldsmith • Class of 1953 • Hoffman Estates, IL

Friends: The June issue of the ANVIL highlighted the remarkable life of a truly remarkable man, Vincent Boryla. The article and added memories were a true pleasure to read, and prompted me to offer a recollection of my own.

I saw the name Vince Boryla and envisioned traditional Friday night pinochle games at our house on Euclid Avenue. My late brother Billy (class of 1944), and my father Max Goldsmith (then the Asst. Chief of Police for East Chicago) would settle in for a regular game, provided it wasn't basketball season, of course. The fourth seat was often left open, and if no unsuspecting soul could be lured into their game, they played "three-handed."

Vince, Dad and Billy were very intense players. This I can recall even though I was only ten years old or so when they would have their games. Vince being a neighbor and close friend of my brother, fit with our family and schmoozed with our father like no one else. The three of them were intense competitors on just about everything, and cards were no exception. They would rarely move, not need to, as our Mother ran in a few drinks and sandwiches.

I can see it as if it were only yesterday. Big Vince finally getting up, and stretching, his broad back and bottom literally soaked from sitting on my Mother's two-inch thick plastic seat covers. He could laugh about it, but my Mother would wonder if the seat covers would ever be right again.

This was many, many years ago, and for the years that followed, my brothers and I always had a good friend in Denver. Vince was as impressive a friend as he is a businessman. Thank you for this opportunity to share a simple memory from simpler times.

Long Walks In The Harbor

Geri (Barloga) Murakowski • Class of 1952 • Munster, IN

Reading Don Kosovac's comments regarding his long lunch-time walks home while attending WHS proved to be a catalyst from my own reminiscing along that line. Don and I were classmates at the time and have remained friends through the years. Now it appears we have our long distance walking memories in common as well. I'm not sure which one of us had the greater distance to and from home, but my marathon lunchtime walks were on a five-day-a-week basis. There were some exceptions, of course. Pouring rain or freezing blizzards usually brought my dad to the rescue with a well appreciated ride. Those times were rare, however, and most of the time I had to depend on my own feet to get me where I had to go.

One corner of my home block of Evergreen Street was adjacent to the prairies. While the prairies served as a marvelous playground and an endless source of childhood adventure and exploration, anyone living in that immediate area had a long walk to WHS. In my own case, it meant six years, two in junior high school and four in high school, of fast-paced long-distance walking.

Once I arrived home for lunch, radio listening, not clock-watching, was the method used to tell the time. It worked perfectly with the three fifteen-minute soap operas involved. Most of the time I rushed through the door during the closing minutes of "Our Gal Sunday," which began at 11:45 am. During "The Romance of Helen Trent" from 12:00 pm until 12:15 pm, I ate my lunch, taking time only to glance at the daily newspaper. "Ma Perkins," at 12:15 pm, signaled that it was time to leave and return to school.

While the time element and lack of interest in the story plots kept me from any real involvement in the shows, I certainly was familiar with the character portrayals and theme

237

music. Since I don't recall ever being late, this system served me well.

Quite a number of WHS students made those long walks four times a day and took it all in stride. Little did we know then that walking would come into such favor and be looked upon as one of the best forms of exercise. I strongly suspect that the long walks I continue to perform daily are a carryover from WHS days. So many years have gone by and I still can't slow down my walking pace.

If now presented with the challenge of repeating that lunchtime marathon walk, could I do it? Years of practice allow me to respond with a firm and clear, "YOU BETCHA!"

Remember the Clubs

Bruce Lax • Class of 1952 • Copperolis, CA

I can't tell you how enjoyable it is to read about WHS, the Harbor, and happenings, current and past. It's great to see familiar names that stir so many fond and lasting memories. Keep up the good work. It was great to read about old friends in Club Olympian via my old friend and schoolmate all the way back to Franklin School and wife of a great guy, Geri (Barloga) Murakowski. During the early 1950s, there were no school-sponsored dances and proms, so clubs like the Olympians, Capitols and Club Esquire sponsored after-the-game and pre-holiday dances at Old and New Croation Halls and yearly proms at Marquette Park. Money for these events was raised from ticket sales and raffles.

Tony Bennett, Nat King Cole, Frank Sinatra, Perry Como, Patti Page, Doris Day, Sarah Vaughn and Billy Eckstine were just a few of the people who sang us through the dances via the old fashioned juke box. The letter from Vince Mroz, re: B.A.B., with his descriptions of the Harbor's ol' swimmin hole, brought tears of pleasant nostalgia. "But the merry days of youth are beyond our control, and it's hard to

238

part forever with the old swimmin' hole."

The letter from Lorraine (Feigenbaum) Cohen, referencing "little brother" Harvey, now a world-class cardiologist, surprising none of us who knew Harvey, was another feel-good gem. It is a source of pride to all WHS alumni when any of the sons and daughters make a mark in the world. References to the Bank Building, Colonel Riley, Dr. Jarabak, "our" bowling alley on Columbus Drive, all the names mentioned as members of the ROMEO club, "Potsy Clark," and all other people, places and happenings mentioned in the ANVIL, triggered a virtual flood of so many golden memories. The building may be gone, but WHS is indestructible. Thank you for keeping it alive.

A Story of Growing Up in Indiana Harbor

Terry Shaffer • Class of 1958 • Naperville, IL

Several weeks ago, when I sent my "where-have-you-been-and-what-are-you-doing now" form sheet back to Anne Marie (promising to send money as soon as I could hustle $35 of my IRS refund), I got this nice little note from Amsie, asking me to write some nostalgia.

How about a true Region love story, one that has withstood the test of time and is today a testimony to the hidden benefits of adolescence among the smokestacks?

It begins some 16 years ago on a summer day, much like today. The pollution count was, maybe, a little higher back then. I had done some traveling around the state and, in Bloomington, I had met a girl named Jo. She lived somewhere south of Ridge Road. Or, as they say in her neighborhood: "A fer piece down th' road." Remember, back in those days (and it still may be true), anyone who lived on the far side of the Route 6 center strip was—to put it politely—a farmer.

Well, Jo thought I was "quaint" with my ducktail, long sideburns, suspenders, vest, padded-shoulder suits and big, black fedora from Milt's Store for Men on Michigan Avenue. I thought she was—uh—words fail me.

The relationship grew, and, finally, I felt she should see from whence I cometh. Spend a weekend with me in Indiana Harbor, I suggested. And bring shoes in case we want to go out somewhere.

When she arrived, she wanted the "local color" tour, so we drove down Michigan Avenue where I pointed out some landmarks: The Auditorium Bar & Grill, Hurwich's Furniture, Harry Tarler's Shoes, Angelo's Supermarket, Larry's Barber Shop and the Busy Corner Drug Store.

That brought us to Pennsylvania Avenue. "It is the dinner hour and I will take you to the Place of the Morning-After Miseries," I said.

"That is a funny name for a restaurant," she said.

"It is a funny restaurant also known as Tacos Joe's," I replied.

The jukebox was playing. Guitars and trumpets. Very colorful. Very local. Senor Joe—which is what I called every Mexican male who worked there—soon brought us a large plate lined with tacos: twelve tortillas wrapped around molten slag. On the side was a pitcher of red brimstone with all those little seeds bobbing around.

"What is that?" she asked, pointing toward the pitcher. "Gravy," I said. "You have to pour it on real thick to get the true flavor."

I thought surely this would even the score for the time she introduced me to hawg jowls and black-eyed peas down at the Steam Corners' Café in her neck of the woods.

She sloshed the sauce across her tacos. Not just a dab here and there, she really poured it on. Her tortillas looked like they were hemorrhaging. With her first bite, her eyes widened and her nostrils flared. She knew she had been had.

"Hot," she said matter-of-factly. She ate two, three, four tacos while I sat waiting for the death scream. "Good," she said smugly. She finished her sixth and began eyeing mine. "You going to eat ALL of those?" she asked. I gobbled mine down while the tears streamed down my cheeks. Very funny, Jo. Ha-ha!

A few weeks later, I got a letter from her. A love letter? Sort of. Boy, did she love those tacos, she wrote. And she asked if I could come down south for a visit. Ah, she did miss me. "By the way, as long as you're coming this way, bring some tacos with you," she said.

At that time, she was living in an apartment in Indianapolis, just a cow's moo away from the Indiana State Fair Grounds. The following weekend, I showed up on her doorstep with a dozen tortillas in one hand and a quart of liquid peppers in the other.

We lived happily ever after.

Epilogue

This story will probably never be made into a movie, but it is an example of the advantages we had in the Harbor. A friend of mine over in Illinois recently asked me: "What is an Indiana Harbor?" A new resort? Something like Bar Harbor, Maine? Sailboats, sunrise, blue skies? Indiana Harbor. Just the name paints a mental picture.

So, I told him about the tin man at Olsen's Sheet Metal Shop across Columbus Drive from the school. The tin man had this big "W" on his chest. The "W" was for Washington High, I said.

"That's Indiana Harbor?" the guy asked. "A tin man with a "W" on his chest?"

See? You can't really explain it to someone who hasn't been there.

You had to live there, grow-up there to know what it is, what it was and what it gave to us. I learned tolerance there. A lot of people who spoke strange languages. Strange aromas floating from kitchen windows. Happy, rocking hymns from the A.M.E. church on 138th Street. But we all learned a simple lesson of survival. We were packed in together into a few square miles, hemmed in by steel mills and oil refineries. We either learned to live together and like it or we packed it up and moved somewhere where everyone was just like us.

If we did that, we cheated ourselves out of a valuable piece of growth. If we run from what we don't understand, we keep on running. In the Harbor, there was precious little room to run so you stayed and you learned to understand. For me, it gave a basis of comparison, a yardstick that will measure all my days.

Today, one of my enjoyments is sitting on a pine-covered hill down in the woods near where Jo grew up. But, when I was growing up, Michigan Avenue or at 139th and Ivy, I learned to love the sound of man-made thunder coming from

the big hammers at the Dickey Forge. Or the rattling of the steel carriers down Euclid Avenue. Or an orange sky on a summer night when Inland was pouring slag.

Both are beautiful: One is quiet beauty; the other powerful.

When we were small, the Harbor seemed big. In size, perhaps it wasn't very large. But in terms of experience, it was a world of our own. It was Johnnie Baratto slamming his blazer to the floor when the referee made a bum call. He was saying, "I'm from the Harbor and we don't have to take it!" Then he'd throw his chair to make his point.

So, here we are, 20 years later—and much the better for it all. Better for having had such a tough, dirty, gritty time when we were kids.

Maybe nobody else knows what the Harbor is, but we do because we lived it, heard it, breathed it's sulphurous air, and watched its burning sky. We know because we're from the Harbor.

Editor's Notes

Mario Martini • Class of 1959 • Highland, IN

On Tuesday May 9, 2000, the ROMEO's met again at Aurelio's on North Calumet Avenue in Hammond. There were about 40 attendees, and all had a very, very good time. Like the last session held in March we just could not let it end at Aurelio's. In March a bunch of us visited the Cavalier's Inn and had some excellent pirogi, and this time we went to the American Legion in East Chicago. We all had a great time, "solved" many problems, advised each other on the merits of many stock tips, and ate and drank all afternoon.

For those who have not attended one of these gatherings of Harbor guys, you are missing out on some great times. Some of those present were Mayor Bob Pastrick, George "Cookie" Van, Abbey Daronatsy, Jim Tchalo, Jack Culver, Joe

Furto, Chuck Nagy, Rich Lokota, Rich Gonzales, Mike Senovic, Joe Pitzel, Alex Akim, Elmer Lucas, Jovan Verce, Ted Stepanovich, Ruben Shehigian, Walt Bulatovich, Dave Field and Larry Field. I apologize to those that were present and were not mentioned in this column. Next time make sure that I have your name on the list.

One of the constant discussions, of course, is about past sporting events at our old school and the feats accomplished forty, fifty and sixty years ago, of course, become great events to be remembered for all time. But one of the more interesting events that occurred at WHS was in 1960. That year John Baratto and the WHS team culminated a great basketball season by capturing the State Tournament title. What memories were evoked by this discussion.

One of the more memorable events of that great season occurred off the court and was not conducted by a member of that great team. You see, Baratto needed scouting information on Muncie Central and its fine players. Well, this is where Jim Tchalo along with Sammy Esposito and Rube Morris enter the story; prior to the final game Jim delivered to the coach one of the finest and greatest scouting reports ever to be given to John Baratto. The following events were related to me by Walt Bulatovich, Abbey and others at Aurelio's.

Jim's report was threefold. First, he told coach that Bonham usually dribbled the ball to about the free throw lane and always backed his way into the opposing center forcing him back and then creating a short shot or lay-up to the basket. He told coach that the first time Ron did that to yell, scream, throw his coat to the floor, and make the officials and the crowd notice Ron's tactic. This was done and as we all know Bonham fouled out for the first time in his career.

Secondly, Bonham and Lampier did not get along at all, and Jim noticed after watching seven or eight of their games that Bonham never threw the ball to Lampier and vice versa. So, Jim suggested to coach to double up guarding on someone else when Lampier or Ron had the ball. Great advice and it worked.

Thirdly, when Davis drove to the basket, it was always down the middle, straight to the basket, so coach told our centers to stand their ground and let Davis run into them. And, of course, this also happened.

And as a result of these three suggestions, all spotted by Jim Tchalo, and the fine and outstanding play of the team, WHS won its first State Championship in basketball. It took forty years for this story to be printed in a publication, but in my opinion and many of those who retell this story, they and John Baratto regarded Jim Tchalo's report as one of the greatest scouting jobs at our school.

Note, the ROMEO's (Retired Old Men Eating Out) outings at Aurelio's are held on the second Tuesday, every other month beginning in January.

Hobo Day was a long-standing tradition at WHS. These are members of the class of 1959; from left, Anne Marie Nedeff, Dave Suban, Joann Mikulaj, Rick Oria, Barbara Yuhasz and Patsy Robinson.

Paul Bramer • Class of 1958 • and
Jeanette Vendramin Bramer • Class of 1956 •
East Chicago, IN

Happy 2000! Hello from da Harbor! I remember walks through the Harbor with my girl, now my wife of 42 years in June (2000) stopping at Carmen's for a Coke and fries. I remember living on Broadway, ice skating at Tod Park, the tennis courts and the duck pond. We had the first prom dance in the new gym. The dance was in the balcony. We had to put paper down on the gym floor for the grand march. This was to keep Coach Baratto happy.

There are many good memories and we still are here in Sunnyside.

Coming Home

Judy (Evans) Church • Class of 1959 • Modesto, CA

Because my two daughters had never seen the area of my childhood, it was such fun to share both rural/urban Indiana and Chicago with them in October (2000). What a joy it was after thirty years to visit with Marion and John Maniotes. Marion and I became good friends the first day I moved into town in 1953 and had our graduation parties together in 1959. The mail has kept us in touch over the years, but there's nothing better than the real thing!

One evening, Marion gave us the royal tour of the "Region," pointing out places familiar (and some not so familiar—she obviously knew the area better than I). The next morning, the girls and I did one more drive to complete the Indiana Harbor part of my "life review" for them . . . the old Girl Scout "Little House" in Tod Park, 139th and Elm.

My ties to the area go beyond my own high school years: my aunt and mother also graduated from East Chicago high schools, my aunt from Roosevelt in 1930, and my mom from WHS in 1928. If anyone wants a copy of the old yearbooks please let me know.

1959 Recollections

Bill Leavitt • Class of 1959 • Merrillville, IN

One of the fond memories I have of old WHS was serving as a movie operator in 1958-1959. My uncle, the famous Carl "Pinkie" Johnson, was in charge of the movies, projectors and screens. Most people knew of Pinkie as a chemistry teacher, and later as assistant principal, but one of his interests was movie equipment.

As his nephew, I was a natural to help him with this important service. Of course, only later did I realize that we movie operators performed a valuable service, helping teachers to use movies as an aid to teaching. Having about twenty student movie operators available permitted a teacher to present movies at any time without tieing up teaching staff. Two of my friends, Dave Suban and Rick Oria (also class of 1959), served in this group of movie operators with me. To me it was a lark. It was a great opportunity to get out of study hall and show a movie. But, the most fun was when one of the other movie operators had a problem. Often I got called out of a real class, like algebra, to help fix the camera or film. That was truly fun!

[Note: Incidentally, my uncle Carl wasn't my only relative involved with WHS. My mother, Violet Johnson Leavitt, graduated in 1927 and substitute taught at WHS in the 50's and 60's; my brother, Don Leavitt, graduated in 1951; my sister, Jo-Ann Leavitt Cobb, graduated in 1962. My uncle Carl "Pinkie" Johnson, and his three children, my uncle, Melvin Johnson, and his three children, and my aunt, Mildred Johnson Feirock, all attended WHS at one time or another.]

Christmas in the Harbor

Ricardo Oria • Class of 1959 • San Antonio, TX

The Harbor years at Christmastime were truly special, starting with the decorations up and down Main Street and Michigan Avenue (Angels and Candy Canes on the light poles). Christmastime meant Christmas Concerts of which me and my good buddy, Willie (Bill Leavitt), were always part of throughout our school years, starting with Riley Elementary with Mr. Law and Miss Lup conducting our band and orchestra. At WHS, Nick Young and Mr. Buckley directed the band and orchestra respectively. Christmas Eve would find Mom in the kitchen preparing her tamales. Wiith the help of my two sisters, Rose Marie and Becky, and neighbors, she would spend Christmas Eve afternoon spreading the masa on corn sheaths. Selecting the perfect tree for $5 was easy since we had several tree lots to choose from (Guthrie Street, Columbus Drive and Main Street). Dad would set up the tree a week before Christmas, and the entire family was involved in its decoration while my sister Rosie played Christmas tunes on the piano. On Christmas Eve, our great thrill was Dad taking us to view the Christmas trees at Inland and Youngstown. We were up early Christmas morning opening gifts; then off to mass at O.L.G. (Our Lady of Guadalupe) Church on Deodar. Christmas in high school years found us dancing to the sound of 'Ziggy," Vintin Santiago and Tony Deja Roasa at Helenic Hall, U.B.M. Hall, Pulaski Post or Croatian Hall. We can't forget those Christmas parties at Cece's and Castro's either. In today's fast, furious and unpredictable world, everybody needs a "Harbor" to reflect back on!

Live and Learn

Rev. Dr. John Zsilvesy • Class of 1954 • El Paso, TX

When I graduated in June, 1954, I didn't know what I would do with my life as I sat on my lifeguard perch at the old Indiana Harbor Beach. My friends were going off to college, and I wasn't. I graduated 178 out of a class of 210, and was ranked at the 68.7 percentile of all high school graduates. (For years, I thought my percentile was in the bottom third.) Later, my wife told me that meant I was in the top third, so I decided to join the U.S. Army. I was alone for the first time in my life, and it didn't frighten me. I had learned how to be confident and cool under pressure while at WHS. We all learned from each other the wisdom gleaned from shared experiences as we came together at WHS, Vince's, Larry's, the Grill or our clubhouse. My study groups were my outstanding WHS classmates and Club 54, a small group of great guys, athletes and mentors.

As I look back, they were my models in areas where I had minimal exposure and experience. They made me feel like I was really somebody as I was slowly developing my personality traits of confidence and coolness in whatever setting. Looking back, my WHS and Club 54 experiences were fantastic. Those experiences proved to be extremely valuable whenever I found myself involved in situations that were beyond my capabilities at that moment. Now, after two retirements, I am actively involved in a fascinating intentional interim ministry and helping to organize the 46th reunion of the class of 1954 for June, 2000. With God, all things are possible. It's true. Look what He did with me.

Harbor Memories

Mario Martini • Class of 1959 • Highland, IN

September 9, 1999, or better known as 9-9-99 to all those te-chies out there, as this is the first date that may signal problems in the upcoming Y2K event. This is the "number day" that I have marked as an event day in my mental diary and "record" for the rest of my life. I well remember the first one, 5-5-55. On that day I was an 8th grader at St. Patrick's Grade School in the Harbor, and looked forward to a good summer and then the start of my high school tenure at WHS. I was really excited at the thought of going to that school; after all, I lived half a block away on Parrish Avenue.

The wonderful memories of those four years at WHS fill my mind and heart with the excitement that we all experienced in that period. The football games at Roosevelt's field, the prom and turnabout dances, the homecoming parties, Hobo Day, the evenings and sometimes days spent at Central Recreation pool hall, pizza at Carmen's, and of course, who can forget the heart-throbbing basketball games at "our new gym," and not playing on the stage at Roosevelt. I remember well when the gym was being built, as we used to scamper up and down the hills of dirt and construction sand, and throw snowballs at passing cars on Grand Boulevard. All scored direct hits, of course. I could never have imagined at that time, the wonderful evenings and days we all would experience during those great years of our champion ECW Senators, from the mid-1950s through the 1960s the 1970s and the 1980s. Of course, we have to single out the years 1960 and 1971, but in my heart, I just cannot forget the great thrills of 1959, my senior year at that great and wonderful school.

We all went on from there to forge our own careers, in all walks of life, but as I experienced at the reunion picnic, we held in August (2000) in Merrillville, and after meeting so many former alumni of all ages, it just impressed me that the common thread we all cannot forget is East Chicago Washington High School and the Harbor!

A Show-Bill Hustler

Mehilo Keseley • Class of 1950 • Ogden Dunes, IN

Having been born and raised in the Harbor was as much a part of my education as the formal part I received at Purdue and IU.

As a 13-year-old I would wake at 6:30 am on Saturday mornings and go to the Indiana Theater. We would wait for the usher to choose the kids that would deliver the show bills for the coming week. We were paid 25 cents and allowed to go to the show three times the following week!

I had many jobs during my high school years: janitor at the Washington Park Pool, washing cars for some of the workers in the "Big House" and working in the park department tending to the flowers.

One of my favorite times involved Club 49 and sponsoring the dances and two senior proms at Marquette Park. I believe these life experiences and the work ethic I learned played an important part in the success I've had as an adult. I know that it's more than I ever imagined growing up on Carey Street in the Harbor!

My wife Marie and I have been married for 45 years and have two terrific children, a son, Louis, 34, and a daughter, Kirsten, 32. We also have two wonderful Springer Spaniels, Winston and Chloe, who share our "empty nest." All in all—a terrific life!

Remembering the Care & Kindness

Elizabeth Sedey • Class of 1950 • Munster, IN

In 1962, the loss of my 19-year-old brother, Louis Ferencz, was a sad and tragic time for our family. During the wake and funeral, Mrs. Georgia Kollintzas came to our house and took charge of the kitchen, preparing food for the family and guests. This was a rather unusual gesture to us since we only knew Mrs. Kollintzas as my brother's friend's mother. The wonderful consideration, care and help of that woman reminded us of what a true neighbor is really supposed to be.

As we were grieving and learning to cope with our loss, Mr. Andy Demantis, who owned the Pool Room on Fir Street, and Alex Akim organized a Benefit Raffle and presented our family with the proceeds. Our family was surrounded by the care of friends that we did not think we had, who were eager to help our family. Thanks again for the fine people of the Harbor. Our family will never forget these kind and generous people.

Class of 1959 Senior Prom was held in the then-new gymnasium.

More Doctors from WHS

Dr. Harvey Feigenbaum • Class of 1951• Indianapolis, IN

Frank: Thank you for publishing the letter from Vanessa Certa, who is an echo technician at St. Anthony Medical Center in Crown Point, IN. It is always nice to know that one's professional efforts are appreciated and have some value. In that same issue of the ANVIL I was delighted to see a brief letter from Jerry Reaven.

Your readers are probably unaware of the fact that Jerry is one of the world's leading endocrinologists, especially in the field of diabetes.

The Reavens and Feigenbaums were actually neighbors in Indiana Harbor.

We lived a half a block apart on Ivy Street. I haven't seen Jerry since he left WHS to enter a combined high school medical school program in Chicago.

However, I was a close friend of his younger brother, Mel, who was only a few weeks older than me. We were both patrol boys in the sixth grade and elected to walk to school together. We kept the routine every day until we graduated from high school in 1951.

Jerry's father had a jewelry store and my father had a men's clothing store, both of which were near the corner of Michigan and Guthrie.

In fact, I purchased my wife's engagement ring from Jerry's father. Unfortunately, Jerry father and brother Mel both died at young ages of heart attacks. I am delighted to see that Jerry is going strong and still active.

Miss Fuhrmark's 1936 Kindergarten Class

(Top Row): Victor Schlossberg, Jack Gaither, Dean Olney,?, ?,
(Second Row): ?, John Pastrick, ? Mehilo Keseley (Third Row): Bill
Alberston, Kenneth Holmes, Steve Chickie.

At ease at Al Dixie's "after hour joint," in East Chicago (138th St. and Main St.) in 1958. From left: Rudy Reyes (class of 1955, legs only showing), Fred Bystricky (class of 1956), Pat Derkacy (class of 1959), Max Fodor (class of 1955), Mel Greiner (class of 1956), Dennis Gronek (class of 1956) and Gene Hauprich (class of 1956).

CHAPTER ELEVEN

11

Memories From the 1960s

In 1965, Lyndon Johnson was the President and Hubert Humphrey was Vice President. The minimum wage was $1.25 and life expectancy was 70.2 years.

The best picture of the year was "The Sound of Music." Lee Marvin was the best actor for his role in "Cat Ballou," and Julie Christy won for "Darling." Some of that decade's popular songs were: "Castles in the Air," "I Will," "I'll Follow the Sun," "I'm Looking Through You," "I've Just seen a Face," "I had a Hammer," "Leaving on a Jet Plane," "Until It's Time to Go" and "Yesterday."

Other interesting data from that year:

Average income	**$6,469.00**
New car	**$2,614.00**
New house	**$13,600.00**
Loaf of bread	**$0.21**
Gallon of gas	**$0.31**
Gallon of milk	**$1 .05**
Gold, per oz.	**$35.00**
Silver, per oz.	**$1.29**
Dow-Jones avg.	**900.00**

From Australia!

Barry Liss • Class of 1960 • Australia

Most people do not quite have a handle on just how far away Australia is. If you send the back issues of the ANVIL by air, I would imagine it would consume a significant portion of your annual budget; and if you send them by sea, we will both have forgotten about them long before they arrive.

Memories of "the Harbor" and WHS: Mostly basketball games and things that happened around basketball games, like stealing the Crown Point Bulldog, going to Indianapolis for the state finals, and mostly just being a kid. That was a fair while ago, though. You would know that, you (Mario Martini, class of 1959) are from the year before me, it says at the bottom of your letter, although to be quite honest, your name does not ring a bell. Another sign of advancing age, I guess.

I ended up in Australia after answering an advertisement in the back of a magazine, "Science," to be precise. I was in the process of finishing a Master's degree in pharmacology in 1970, and the University of Queensland was advertising for staff. I got the job, loved the place and have lived here ever since. It is unlikely that I will be in a position to attend any of the gatherings, such as the ones that you have described. I think that the best time that I have ever made for the trip was approximately 25.5 hours (good connections and a tail wind across the Pacific). Actual flying time, Chicago to Brisbane, is just on nineteen hours. A direct flight does not exist, however, and with stops in Sydney and California, the time increases. One does not just drop in.

Thank you again for the email and for jostling my memory. I haven't thought about those days in a long time, and it felt good. As I understand it, John Gustaitis is back in "The Region," and John Evon never left. They, and Mike

Goodman, were my closest friends from that period, and I still keep in touch with Mike.

Music at WHS

Nanci J. Elish • Class of 1960 • Simi Valley, CA

I loved attending WHS. I played the violin. I remember Mr. Buckley for conducting the orchestra and Dean Croxton for choral music and the fabulous "Hi Lites," in which I got to perform dance! Larry Kulig was my partner. I remember Tony Carr performing the Warsaw Piano Concerto. I also remember Mrs. Sutton for the production of fabulous plays. The music teachers at Washington Elementary, Mr. Paul Posh, and at WHS, Mr. Charles Buckley, helped me win several first place honors performing at the Double Bach Violin Concert with Mischa Vajagich, who now lives in Germany.

I also remember when we won the State Basketball Championship in 1960! I screamed so much, due to being excited, I had a sore throat for several days. Also, my WHS tee-shirt, being maroon, was stained pink from the excitement. The word sure got out when we won the State Championship—I invited 20 people to our house—4213 Ivy. Basketball players, cheerleaders and friends, over 200 students came from all over the Calumet Area!! From Morton, Highland, Hammond H.S., etc. We served over 200 Cokes, and my dad had to go to Kroger's to get more (10 loaves bread, 20 lbs. boiled ham and potato salad). We danced the "horse" then.

Well, we tried to write some memories. Best wishes to you!

Looking Back

Michael Goodman • Class of 1960 • Westport, CT

When you make your living as a corporate strategic planning consultant, you spend all of your time looking ahead 3-5 years, so it was a real shocker to receive a few copies of the new ANVIL, and be thrust backward 40 years, through a time warp, to Indiana Harbor and WHS.

To get the juices flowing again, I unpacked the box with high school and college memorabilia and found—get this—a stack of SENATORIAL issues from 1956 to 1959! For those of you whose memory is even worse than mine, the SENATORIAL was our school newspaper [formerly the WEEKLY ANVIL—Ed.], and it was hand-set in Mr. Kincaid's print shop by those of us who found that now-obsolete craft interesting. (Remember when we had to memorize the locations of each letter in a California job case?) During most of the period from 1956 to 1959, the journalism teacher (and advisor to the SENATORIAL staff) was Mrs. Vann, and she was one of the "newbies" back then.

Mrs. Vann also taught typing, and I often think back, as I curse my computer keyboard, to those heavy, manual typewriters with no letters printed on the keys. Who could have guessed that touch-typing would become such an important skill? Now kids go to a computer lab and rely on Mavis Beacon (on a CD-ROM) to get to a level that would have made Mrs. Vann think that we were somehow cheating as we typed out "a";sldkfjghfjdksla;" over and over and over.

One of the first memories to hit me as I flipped through the yellowed pages of that stack of old newspapers (if you can call them that) was an event that invoked my homeroom and our homeroom teacher, Miss Mendenhall. Jessie Mendenhall was a wonderful woman and a gifted math teacher who touched the life of every student who walked into her classroom. I remember her taking roll to see who was present/absent, and having some of the more imaginative students come up with novel responses like "present physically, Miss Mendenhall" or "I made it in today." I particularly remember David Derkacy, Tim Simon (the son of Dan Simon, who was principal of WHS for several years) and Billy Fox (also the son of an East Chicago School System principal, John Fox) trying to see how far they could go to be entertaining.

Janet Biederstadt (Klepsch) • Class of 1962 • Bellingham, WA

Greetings from the great Pacific Northwest. I can't tell you the joy and the warm feelings drawn while reading the ANVIL. As my husband Bob, a TFS 1959 graduate reminds me, "you can take the girl out of the Harbor, but not the Harbor out of the girl." And boy am I proud of that fact! Harbor people are unique. Each issue of the ANVIL reminds all of us "Harbor Kids" how lucky we were to have been raised there. Thank you, Frank, for your labor of love and for keeping the memories alive. God Bless!

WHS Class of 1961 Reunion

By: Bill Leavitt • Class of 1959 • Merrillville, IN

I attended the Class of 1961 Reunion in October even though I am from the class of 1959. Like many WHS alumni, I have many friends in other classes. I must say it was very enjoyable for me, and a great success for all class of 1961 attendees. They had a turnout of 119, of which 74 were class members and 10-15 were from the classes of 1959, 1960 and 1962. The group was extremely hospitable. In fact I not only saw many old friends who I had not seen in over 40 years, but made some new friends. I heartily recommend attending reunions of classes other than your own. The reunions are often listed in the ANVIL, as well as in local newspapers.

What impressed me most about the reunion was the way the Class of 1961 Committee made the trip more worthwhile for out-of-town class members. Instead of traveling a long way for just one event, the Class of 1961 Committee planned three events. Also, two of the events were free-of-charge, so no local classmate could complain about the cost. Friday night was a hors d'eorves and open-bar reception at the Robert A. Pastrick Marina in Indiana Harbor. It was free (subsidized by the Saturday evening banquet at the same location). On Sunday, class members and guests attended a brunch.

Saturday night was the main event, a dressy dinner with entertainment, dancing and lots of time to catch up with long-absent classmates. I personally saw at least ten old friends who I hadn't seen in 40-42 years.

When you go to your own class reunion, you often see the same people time after time. Depending on how frequently you have them, you may see your classmates every five years, ten years, fifteen years, etc. Yet when you go to the reunion of another class besides your own, you may be seeing people that you haven't seen since the day you left high school. What a thrill to see people after all those years.

Since I'm not from the class of 1961, the success of the events is more appropriately judged by seeing what some of the attendees said about it. I invited several attendees to give their impressions of the class reunion. Those impressions follow my article. Arliss Kozlowski Beardmore, Julio Torres, Peggy McNealy Smith, George Richard Angulano and Carolyn Guthrie Bryson are represented below. Arliss came all the way from Vancouver, British Columbia (in Canada); Julio from Baytown, Texas; Peggy from Valparaiso; George from San Antonio, Texas; and Carolyn from Beach Park, Illinois. Also, one member of the class of 1961, Ed Clark of Gary, wrote a poem.

Arliss (Kozlowski) Beardmore •
Vancouver, British Columbia, Canada

When I opened the invitation to the class reunion my immediate reaction was "Yes!" I was excited and really looking forward to it. I began making plans and telling my friends about the upcoming event. Their responses surprised me. It was universally regarded as a bad idea to attend one's class reunion. As I listened to horror stories about other people's experiences, I began to reconsider. I was so disheartened that I stopped making arrangements to travel.

September 11th changed everything. After what happened that day, I knew I had to come "home" to the USA to reconnect with my American identity. I'm glad I did. It was great to see the Harbor again and the not-so-familiar faces of my former classmates. The organizing committee did a wonderful job arranging the location, food, entertainment, prizes, reunion photo and everything else that made it such a memorable occasion. While in the area, I spent time with family members who I had not seen since 1990, visited with an old friend, the only classmate I have stayed connected with over the years, and I played the tourist in downtown Chicago. Now that I have experienced what it's like, I will have my own advice to give to others who may be contemplating a class reunion. My advice is to them is "Go!" The longer you have been away, the more important it is to attend. I want to offer a special thank you to whoever it was that tracked me down and sent me the invitation to the reunion. I wouldn't have missed it for anything.

Julio Torres • Baytown, TX

Everyone I have talked to after the reunion felt that this reunion was the best that we have ever had. It was great seeing everyone, but especially the ten or more people who were there for the first time since we left high school.

I believe our reunion committee did a great job of getting it all together. I'm already looking forward to next August 24th weekend when we will get together again.

I talked to one member who we had lost contact with for the last 40 years, and he is going to make a big effort to be there in August. I also talked to some of our classmates who did not attend this year for one reason or another, and they too are looking forward to being there this time. I am certain that next August's get-together is going to be even better than this year's reunion.

From Peggy (McNealy) Smith • Valparaiso, IN

Looking back over my previous reunions, my 40th-year reunion was by far the "best ever." The food and the festivities were excellent, and the reunion was well planned. Beginning Friday night, which was casual night, I was happy to see many classmates for the first time since graduation.

It was a great pleasure reminiscing about our "favorite and not so favorite" teachers. It was encouraging seeing the success of many of our classmates. Many WHS grads have populated much of the United States and parts of Canada. We have graduates who came from as far as Oregon, Texas and Vancouver, Canada. This is a tribute to WHS and to the teachers who prepared us for life after high school.

The second night of the reunion was "Dress-Up Night." Everyone was dressed to "impress." The men looked handsome and the women beautiful. Everyone had a great time. The gifts were plentiful, and class members and guests alike received a token of the reunion.

The videotaped interview was a new and bright idea. I am looking forward to receiving my copy and listening to the comments of my classmates. This will be my fondest keepsake of this wonderful reunion. The comradery was great—and fun was had by all!!

George Richard Angulano • San Antonio, TX

I guess we've all returned from the reunion and settled back into our daily routines. I wanted to wait a while before sending this email for that very reason. Once your life is back to normal, I can then feel comfortable in sending all of you my feelings regarding the WHS Class of 1961 reunion on the weekend of October 18, 19 and 20.

First and foremost, I want to applaud the reunion committee—Barbara Serbon (Padgett), Sharon Molnar (Holajter), Linda Dix (Byrd), Frank Kollintzas, David Sunny, Jerry Engle, Manuel Ortiz, Ed Clark, Henry Borom, Robert Carter, Toribio Garza and anyone else involved——for an extraordinary effort in what turned out to be one of the most memorable weekends of my life. Sure, some of you may think, "If that weekend was the best time of his life, he surely must have led a sheltered life." But, I say to you cynics, in the past 40 years since I left my hometown of East Chicago (The Harbor) I've circumvented the world many times and in the process worked or lived in 18 different countries. I've written a novel while raising my two youngest children (now young adults) as a single parent and have battled and beat cancer. It's been a tough road with many potholes, sharp curves and detours; although a few nice rest spots have been thrown in along the way.

The main point of this email is not to toot my own horn, but to convey to you that, for me personally, no matter how far and for how long you wander from your home roots, home is still home.

I was, like many of you, born and raised in the Harbor. I left home out of high school to attend college in California, returning only sporadically to visit family. My weekend back home this last October would have been just that—another visit back home. What made it so wonderful was you. Seeing all of you again—some for the first time in 40 years—was remarkable. It brought me back to my youth. The corridors of my mind became filled with memories of dating, sports, fun, high school and old friends. That kind of weekend can't be bought through a travel agent, nor purchased at any store. It's simply priceless. Seeing all of you again will remain a precious part of my thoughts, and I can't wait to see you all again at our next gathering.

For those of you who missed this year's reunion, please try and make it to the next. I promise you, you'll have a wonderful time. Until then, Ciao!

Carolyn (Guthrie) Bryson • Beach Park, IL

I want to tell you how much I enjoyed the 40th reunion celebration. It was great to be back in the Harbor and to see so many people I had not seen in 40 years. I was really glad Julio called me soooo many times to "encourage" me to attend! Everything was so tastefully done, everything. You guys did a terrific job.

E. C. WASHINGTON'S MONUMENT

By Ed Clark • Class of 1961 • Gary, IN

"They've torn down Washington," I heard them say
and on that sad and infamous day.
My heart recoiled in misery
'til my pulse reminded me . . .
We are Washington's living legacy.

"They've torn down Washington," but consider this
. . . in memories it still exists.
We don't deny its walls are gone . . .
But, with our next breath . . . the school lives on
and after we are rendered dust . . .
one generation more is held in trust
And so, while one heart still beats
its demolition is incomplete.

"They've torn down Washington," they still say . . .
and they'll replace it in a day . . .
with all the latest technology
in a new Central facility.
I've walked its halls . . . I'm not impressed
by a cold facade of brick and glass
and student's eyes that contemptuously
reject Washington's sense of propriety.

"They've torn down Washington" . . . why I asked?
Our school was more then brick and glass
and much more then the sum of its parts
Washington High School had a heart.

"They've torn down Washington," what a sad refrain
as if our school was just a name.
It had a spirit sixty years sublime . . .

which transcended plans and design.
Through generations of eager minds
imbued with a sense of integrity
and inspired by a committed faculty—build in that . . . with
your technology!

"They've torn down Washington," they still insist.
but I suggest . . . you remember this:

"Build new schools . . .
and you build them high!
Let their towers scrape the sky.
Then tear them down
. . . they will be gone . . .
that's not the fate of Washington."

So we, the Class of '61, do celebrate and reaffirm
all the things that we have learned
in memories of those halcyon days
when Washington stood straight and tall
molding three generations of us all . . .
with a creed that remains intact:
   " . . . I represent my school in
   every word and act . . ."
We are now its embodiment as a physical fact.

CHAPTER Twelve
12

Saying Goodbye to WHS

Underground ANVIL

Out-takes From Forgotten ANVILs

Constance Barnes (MacMillen) ('33), now of Highland, once bought a stunning designer label dress from Lewin's new Store for Women. It was called basic black by Miss Mann.

After attending the American Conservatory and the Chicago Musical College, Miss Grace L. Boyce came to Indiana Harbor where she became a virtuoso on the scissors grinder.

According to Mary Ben (Young) ('36), now of Munster, the gypsies encamped at Cudahy worked out a joint venture with Tepper's Hock Shop.

Ione Williams ('38), now of Lake of the Four Seasons and once a habitué of the Busy Bee Confectionary, reports that Larry Laidella had to send out his change apron for carbon dating.

George Nicksic ('34), now of Schererville, insists that Mamie Overpeck told a class that she would flunk the next pupil who insisted that the Figure 8 was the sum of 3311.

John Hlavaty ('38), now of Canton, OH, swears that only myopics were allowed on Lake Front Beach while Mamie Kirilova ('39) and Norma Jean Spector ('39) sought all-over suntans on the Intake.

Gayle Tolf (Farmer) ('45), now of Munster, vehemently denies that her Marktown enclave was a Communist cell, even while admitting that children there frequently played Red Rover.

Garland Criswell ('45), now a retired minister in Peoria, IL, relentlessly campaigned for the morals of Harbor youth by demanding that the popular beach game "Baby In The Hole" be banned after dark.

Billy Corder ('45), Emmy-winning TV producer and now of Ada, MI, said that Police Officer Nichols conveyed 10,000 children across 141st Street, and still sold his 1,000th ticket to the non-existent Policeman's Ball.

Jerry Melongoni ('43), former Mr. Washington and tankman supreme, reported that Hammond High severed relations with WHS when the Senators scheduled a dual meet in the General American whirlpool.

Twice-wounded John Galambos ('64), president of Griffith's school board, reported that the American Legion proclaimed racial balance had been achieved in the Harbor when Harbison Walker caused just as much black lung disease as Universal-Atlas caused white lung disease.

On behalf of all Harbor shift workers, musician Elizabeth Mosny ('49), now of Houston, presented the bells of the Romanian Orthodox Church on Elm Street with the annual Quazimoto Award.

According to novelist Leslie Edgeley ('30), now of Los Angeles, the Grand Boulevard library is famous not only for its giant flower pots out front, but its deflowered librarians below.

Thermal experts Jean McClure (Williams) ('44), now of Griffith, and Violet Chulay (Manuszak), now of Goleta, CA, testified that the ice skating hot house was air conditioned compared to the balcony of the Indiana Theater.

Highland's George Elish ('43), the peerless southpaw

pitcher, swears that scout executive Arthur J. Sambrook was often arrested for impersonating Groucho Marx.

Carl Trimble, now of Lakewood, CO, reported that the 141st Street viaduct was extended so that the Harbor could conduct a Soap Box Derby, despite warnings from Mayor Rooney that anyone entering the Rinso Box from atop Lever Brothers would be severely dealt with.

Bernard Solberg ('32), now of Nokomis, FL, said that Councilman Meyer Lipner had started a campaign to have the Pennsy Block area designated a Historic District.

While researching accident prevention, Dr. John Meyer, now of Beverly Shores, found that Packy Maugher, the Auditorium saloonist, had contributed to workplace accidents by sponging up spilled drinks from his bar and discounting the slops to WPA workers leaning on shovels.

Legionnaire Frank Hanak ('38), WHS Alum chair and now of Griffith, once gave a fair hiring award to Post 266 for employing a wall full of one-armed bandits. Len Hedinger ('44), now of Dyer, first earned his reputation as "life of the party" when he borrowed a John McGuan prop better known as Jimmie, the Mummie.

On behalf of a Women's Rights group, Irene Kwiecien (Mackowiak), now of East Chicago, criticized Sherpetosky's Dance Studio, claiming that Bessie Shep was turning out contortionists who could twist themselves into so many shapes that their husbands could make love to them and cheat on them at the same time.

Deep-thinking Kenneth Kovack, a union lobbyist now of Rockville, MD, once arranged for a fellow philosopher to pose to the WHS Senior Assembly this question: "If a man speaks in a forest and there's no woman there to criticize him, is the man still wrong?"

According to John Farmer ('41), now of Munster, Freddie Brenman, when questioned about his source of income, said he did everything by the numbers.

Richard Lax ('45), now of Grand Junction, CO, reported that incorrigible pupils who did not make the cut for Mr. Russell Richey's basket-weaving class were forthwith assigned to the monkey house of the Washington Park Zoo.

Mildred Gorman (Kennedy) ('38), now of N. Brandford, CT, said that Superintendent Roy Feik decreed that the side shows of the school carnival added up to another version of night school.

Fred Stockhaus ('39), one of WHS's all-time great pitchers and linemen, appeared as a character witness during the deposing of Thomas Altenderfer, Raymond Frankenhauser, Gladys Freudenreich, R.C. Rencenberger, Jessie Mendenhall, Nick Brunswick and Adolph Schweingruber, all of whom swore they were not members of WHS's German-American Bund.

Ed Nemeth ('44), quarterback of WHS's 1942 state football champions, brought down the house during the Minstrel Show, but when cast members became unruly reported with them to Mr. Robinson's office for questioning. Big Bob began the interview with: "Just think of me as Mr. Interlocutor."

The Last Hurrah at Washington High School

Bob Krajewski • Class of 1946 • Munster, IN

The idea of having an alumni farewell party for both WHS and RHS was an intriguing approach to the problem of some lingering community discontent over the decision to replace the two high schools. With some concern, the school board gave the go ahead. It turned out to be a smashing success. On April 30, 1986, we had the final farewell to Washington High School. The gym was almost packed to capacity with old alums saying goodbye to a community treasure that had served so many thousands of students. The building rocked with music, cheers and song. Many of us recall that replacing WHS and RHS with a new high school was not an easy sell.

Many remembered the schools as they were 20, 30, even 50 years ago, and few had been back to see how decayed and outmoded the institutions had become. So, we decided to use those old memories to draw people together, let them see how their old alma maters had aged, and turn their reluctant acceptance of a new school into support. Planning the events at both schools started with involving a broad-based community group of 65 enthusiastic volunteers. They got

HARBOR HIGHLIGHTS:
The Last Hurrah at Washington High School, April 30, 1986

IT CERTAINLY WAS A GRAND OLD SCHOOL!

the word out with an extensive public campaign using news releases, radio interviews and mailings. An anonymous grad donated several hundred dollars to purchase newspaper ads. The schools printed 3,500 flyers which the committee distributed. We used incentives to boost attendance: We took orders for bricks from the old buildings for $1.00, proceeds for new band uniforms; we announced the sale of old yearbooks, banners, T-shirts and other memorabilia; refreshments would be available. Despite all of our planning for Alumni Nite, we were concerned about the turnout. However, when the first alums to arrive included an elderly man on crutches and another using a walker, we knew we had a winner. The program flyer indicated that the building was open for touring at 6:00 pm, and individual rooms were assigned for each decade, beginning with the 1920s, to visit and review memorabilia. The building was mobbed! The very short program was scheduled for 7:30 pm. The band began playing in the main building leading the stragglers into the gym.

As the band entered, playing "Hail, Noble Washington," the crowd rose with a roar; it was goose-bump time. After short introductory remarks, a representative from each of the decades from the 1920s through the 1980s spoke briefly about what WHS meant to them. The program ended with a final rousing rendition of the school song; refreshments were then served. It was an absolutely inspiring evening! By the way, Roosevelt had their Alumni Nite the evening before. It too, was a success. Over 6,500 attended the two events.

Washington High School Administrative Staff and Teachers and Their Subject Assignments 1985-1986

Nick Ranich - Principal
John Flores - Vice Principal
Doloris Lakich - Assistant Principal
Lawrence Webb - Faculty Representative in Charge of Student Discipline.
June Cravens - Counselor
Frank Kopanda - Counselor
Martin Quinn - Counselor
Sylvia Morrisroe - Counselor

Darnell Adell - Special Education
Myra Anderson - Foreign Language
Adelaida Aquino - English
Peter Auksel - Math
Shirley Bailey - Physical Education
Luanrie Bloos - English
Travis Buggs - Physical Education
Victoria Candelaria - Foreign Language
Elaine Carpenter - School Nurse
Julianne Collins - Math
Louise Comer - Foreign Language
Paul Demkovich - English
Lillian Eldridge - Special Education
John Fife - Audio Visual
Cavanaugh Gary - Ind. And Voc. Arts
William Gaskey - Business Education
Joyce George - Math
Robert George - Math
George German - Math
Thomas Hardaway - Art
Paul Hric - Social Science
James Hughes - Natural Science
Dwane Jackett - Natural Science
Maria Jalocha - Math
Frances Jeney - Business Education
John Johnson - Art
Leon Kendrick - Music
Linda Kincaid - Special Education
June Kosanovich - English
Lawrence Lane - Music
Ignatius Leal - Natural Science
Mary Lenaburg - Special Education
Frank Lichtenstein—English
Frank Lucas - Natural Science
Arthur Martinmaki - Music

Eli Matovich - English
Barbara Mauger - Home Economics
Gloria McCumber - Business Education
Walter Metcalf - Natural Science
Nikki Mik - School Nurse
Dominic Mikutis - Math
William Morris - Physical Education
Ava Mosely - Home Economics
James Mulcahey - English
Ruth Naumoff - Social Science
Betty Lou Oberg - Home Economics
Donald Palla - Social Science
Carolyn Parker - Art
Charles Parker - Social Science
Bradford Piniak - Social Science; Physical Education
Natalie Radich - English
Armando Reyes - Special Education
Anita Ryan - Art
Robert Segovia - TESOL
James Sidenbender - Speech
Jules Siegle - Physical Education
June Simmons - Physical Education
Rudolph Smith - Business Education
Ronald Soverly - Social Science
Sylvia Vucich - Library
Steve Wargo - Social Science
Donald Wilson - English

Schoolrooms to Bedrooms

On April 20, 1999, a ground-breaking ceremony was held at the site of our former school. Speakers included: Mayor Robert A. Pastrick; Councilman Frank Kollintzas, 4th District; Michael Pannos, East Chicago Second Century; George Dawkins, Washington High School Review Committee.

Sixty-eight homes ranging in price from $112,000 to $158,000 will be built in a park-like setting on what most of us consider hallowed ground. This development will transform the barren ground created by razing our school into one of the finest residential areas in town.

The underground work has begun. Backhoes are

digging trenches and bulldozers have already removed the wire fencing from around what was the athletic field and ice skating rink. You remember that fence, don't you? How many of us were introduced to it wintertime when we were stupid enough to end up at the tail-end position of "Crack the Whip."

A central pavilion and plaza area is planned for the heart of development. Pocket parks will be created for green space, and a walking path will encircle the development. Among the new street names chosen are: Senator Lane, Anvil Lane and Maroon Lane.

E. C. WASHINGTON'S MONUMENT

By Ed Clark • Class of 1961 • Gary, IN

"They've torn down Washington," I heard them say
and on that sad and infamous day.
My heart recoiled in misery
'til my pulse reminded me . . .
We are Washington's living legacy.

"They've torn down Washington," but consider this
. . . in memories it still exists.
We don't deny its walls are gone . . .
But, with our next breath . . . the school lives on
and after we are rendered dust . . .
one generation more is held in trust
And so, while one heart still beats
its demolition is incomplete.

"They've torn down Washington," they still say . . .
and they'll replace it in a day . . .
with all the latest technology
in a new Central facility.
I've walked its halls . . . I'm not impressed
by a cold facade of brick and glass
and student's eyes that contemptuously
reject Washington's sense of propriety.

"They've torn down Washington" . . . why I asked?
Our school was more then brick and glass
and much more then the sum of its parts
Washington High School had a heart.

"They've torn down Washington," what a sad refrain
as if our school was just a name.
It had a spirit sixty years sublime . . .

which transcended plans and design.
Through generations of eager minds
imbued with a sense of integrity
and inspired by a committed faculty—build in that . . . with
your technology!

"They've torn down Washington," they still insist.
but I suggest . . . you remember this:

"Build new schools . . .
and you build them high!
Let their towers scrape the sky.
Then tear them down
. . . they will be gone . . .
that's not the fate of Washington."

So we, the Class of '61, do celebrate and reaffirm
all the things that we have learned
in memories of those halcyon days
when Washington stood straight and tall
molding three generations of us all . . .
with a creed that remains intact:
   ". . . I represent my school in
   every word and act . . ."
We are now its embodiment as a physical fact.